Migration

Titles in this series

Zygmunt Bauman, *Community: Seeking Safety in an Insecure World*

Zygmunt Bauman, *Globalization: The Human Consequences*

Norberto Bobbio, *Left and Right: The Significance of a Political Distinction*

Alex Callinicos, *Equality*

Diane Coyle, *Governing the World Economy*

Andrew Gamble, *Politics and Fate*

Paul Hirst, *War and Power in the 21st Century*

Bill Jordan and Franck Düvell, *Migration: The Boundaries of Equality and Justice*

James Mayall, *World Politics: Progress and its Limits*

Ray Pahl, *On Friendship*

Shaun Riordan, *The New Diplomacy*

Migration

The Boundaries of Equality and Justice

BILL JORDAN

and

FRANCK DÜVELL

polity

First published in 2003 by Polity Press in association with Blackwell Publishing Ltd

Editorial office:
Polity Press
65 Bridge Street
Cambridge CB2 1UR, UK

Marketing and production:
Blackwell Publishing Ltd
108 Cowley Road
Oxford OX4 1JF, UK

Distributed in the USA by
Blackwell Publishers Inc.
Commerce Place
350 Main Street
Malden, MA 02148, USA

A catalogue record for this book is available from the British Library.

Library of Congress Cataloging-in-Publication Data
Jordan, Bill, 1941–
Migration: the boundaries of equality and justice / Bill Jordan and Franck Düvell.
p. cm.—(Themes for the 21st century)
Includes bibliographical references and index.
ISBN 0-7456-3007-3—ISBN 0-7456-3008-1 (pbk.)
1. Emigration and immigration—Government policy. 2. Emigration and
immigration—Moral and ethical aspects. 3. Emigration and immigration—Social
aspects. 4. Globalization. I. Düvell, Franck, 1961. II. Title. III. Series.
JV6038 .J67 2003
325′.1—dc21
2002014150

Typeset in 10.5 on 12 pt Plantin
by SetSystems, Saffron Walden, Essex
Printed in Great Britain by T.J. International, Padstow, Cornwall

Contents

Preface and Acknowledgements   vii

1   Introduction: Issues and Perspectives   1

2   The New Model of Global Governance   27

3   The Political Economy of Migration   59

4   Cosmopolitan Economic Membership   91

5   Global Equality and Justice   124

Notes   157

Index   182

Preface and Acknowledgements

At the start of the new century, migration and borders have emerged as unresolved issues for governance. The rise of anti-immigrant parties in such leading democracies as Australia, Denmark and the Netherlands, inter-ethnic conflicts in the Middle East and South Asia, and the plight of refugees worldwide all signal problems for political liberalism and the international order.

This book sets these issues in the context of an integrated world economy, with new means of mobility and new boundaries of membership. Corporations produce, sell and recruit without regard for national borders. States accommodate new forms of cosmopolitan nomadism, and open their collective infrastructures for transformation by market agents. International organizations monitor for 'state failure', and the world hegemon ponders 'regime change' through military intervention.

So our aim is to analyse migration and its management as one of the themes of globalization, and linked to those of sustainable development, the transformation of post-communist societies, and relations between rich and poor states. We argue that all these issues demand a theory of boundaries, which is at present lacking in political and social thought. We criticize social scientific and philosophical models of mobility and membership, and investigate alternative ethical analyses of the bases for equality and justice.

We take this opportunity to thank a number of people who have helped greatly in the preparation of this book. First, we are grateful to Professor Bo Stråth of the European University Institute, Florence, and our colleagues in the EC-funded IAPASIS research project, during the course of which some of the material in chapter 3 was gathered. We also warmly thank the managers and staff of Work Permits (UK), who helped us recruit some of the interviewees quoted there; Emilia Breza, who conducted some of the interviews; and the interviewees themselves for talking to us.

We especially acknowledge our gratitude to colleagues who read and commented on the first draft of all, or parts, of the book, most notably Rainer Bauböck, Michael Breuer, Alan Carling, Phillip Cole and Toru Yamamori. We take full responsibility for remaining errors.

Finally, we are very grateful to Gill Watson and Di Cooper for their efficiency in preparing the typescript.

1

Introduction:
Issues and Perspectives

The new world order is a disappointment. Since the collapse of the Soviet Bloc regimes, it has been possible to imagine a global system of security, prosperity and justice in which conflicts could be resolved, economic growth sustained and all the people of the world gain access to the resources (income, education, health care) for a good life. Instead, this vision is mocked by war, ethnic strife, economic insecurity and starvation at the start of the new century.

Globalization, the set of forces that makes populations more interdependent, also divides them. A defining feature of the integration of the world economy is movement of all kinds across organizational boundaries. As a special instance of this, the accelerated movement of people across political borders (migration) has a strongly disputed significance. It can be taken as a signal of at least four different problems of the new world order.

1 *The need for stronger national sovereignty.* In this view, nation states are still the most viable systems for security, membership and social justice; hence border controls are necessary features of the international order. Inward migration is a threat because it can overwhelm collective infrastructures, lay waste environments and destroy cultures, provoking civil disorder. Without such controls, no

state has a motive to provide inclusive equality and justice for its citizens, since each could expel its minorities, dump its poor and empty its prisons into neighbour countries.[1] From this perspective, unauthorized immigrants are virtual criminals; some have even argued that mass migrations are akin to acts of war.[2]

2 *The need for more effective international governance.* In this view, global economic integration demands a stronger role for international organizations, in steering financial stability, managing growth and preventing poverty. Agencies like the International Monetary Fund, the World Bank and the World Trade Organization can set the structural conditions under which these goals can best be achieved. Migration is a problem in so far as it involves 'externalities' – costs generated by economic agents who do not compensate those who lose through their activities – such as 'brain drains' and congestion.[3] Hence such agencies as the International Organization for Migration can play an important role in systems for managing movements of population.

3 *The emergence of new systems of membership.* From this perspective, new means of mobility, and new organizational boundaries, have contributed to a declining relevance of existing political communities. Increased migration flows signal the need for a reappraisal of the appropriate role, size and composition of each level of political authority. Hence the problem may lie in the existing pattern of jurisdictions, rather than the mobility of people, which could drive forward improved efficiency in the provision of collective services.[4] Migration might, in fact, be an instrument of political transformation, helping all to benefit from globalization.[5]

4 *New vulnerabilities and new needs for social protection.* In this view, increasing inequality and poverty worldwide demand new institutional structures for social justice to

replace welfare states. These must include systems of distribution and provision that take account of increased mobility. Accelerated migration is a warning, signalling the destabilization of systems of membership, and the intensification of injustices, especially in the developing world.[6]

Each of these views on migration also represents a distinctive interpretation of the nature and implications of globalization. The first ('neo-Hobbesian nationalist') has been surprisingly influential on the politics of such diverse states as Australia, the Netherlands and Denmark. The second is reflected in both the Washington Consensus version of the new world order and recent modifications to it ('Globalization with a Human Face').[7] The third ('fiscal federalism and the economic theory of clubs') is derived from theoretical analysis; it has influenced public finance and the transformation of public services all over the world, and underpins the proposals for a General Agreement on Trade in Services (GATS). The fourth ('transnational ethics') informs the campaigns of many international non-government organizations (NGOs) and local community groups.[8] For convenience, these names will be abbreviated to the *nationalist*, *globalist*, *federalist* and *ethical* perspectives.

So this is not simply a book about migration, but one that investigates the crossing of borders within a more general context of mobility between systems of membership. Such an analysis requires a theory of *boundaries*; borders are a specific kind of boundary, between political communities. We argue that boundary problems are a theme for the twenty-first century, and migration policies provide one way of focusing on these.

The right to join organizations of all kinds was an essential element in the semi-successful emancipations of the twentieth century – of women, the working classes and ethnic minorities. The freedom to choose where to live and work was central to these mobilizations, as the bastions of power and privilege were opened up to new members. But rights of access and freedom of movement are not ends in themselves. They are valuable in so far as they allow membership organizations to be transformed, according to principles of equality and justice.

These principles, in turn, are ultimately related to ideals of human co-operation – imagined utopias where members contribute voluntarily, to the best of their potential, to activities that meet the needs of all, and that allow them to negotiate fairly about common purposes, but leave them free to pursue their own. Rules for entry and exit would therefore be integral parts of these membership systems.

In this book, we use the general term *mobility* to indicate the capacity to leave and enter organizations, including that for physical movement between jurisdictions. Hence this term embraces forms of mobility that are characteristic of globalization, such as electronic transfers. Agents can change allegiance from one fund, firm, brand or club to another, without moving away from their computer screens.

We use the term *membership* to denote inclusion in any organization (a system of membership) that is capable of providing goods, services or other benefits to those who belong to it, and excluding those who do not, where belonging may involve allegiances acquired by birth, affiliation, entry or subscription. Again, joining and leaving such organizations may or may not require a physical shift in location. Membership systems may be formal or informal. It is their collective aspect that distinguishes mobility in our sense (entering and exiting such systems) from trade in private goods or going on holiday.

The concept of *migration* is more difficult to define

unambiguously. In its original meaning, it simply described people moving, as fish, birds and animals do, under forces of nature, often following their flocks in search of pasture. Such nomads posed a problem for rulers when states were formed, because they continued to cross national boundaries after land and its resources had been transformed into *territory* by the formation of political communities. We reserve the term 'migration' for the movement of people across borders, both by choice and under economic and political forces,[9] which involves stays of over a year. This means that internal population movements and short-term trips for business, study or tourism are treated as 'geographical mobility' in this text. The diversity of forms of migration will be explored in chapter 3. In the next section we will consider how the primacy of nation states as systems of membership came to be challenged by the actions of economic organizations. In chapter 4, we will analyse how this has given rise to new forms of nomadism.

The political economy of globalization

In order to clarify how the integration of the world economy has transformed membership systems, we should first outline what it was that was being transformed, and which agents were mainly responsible for the transformation.

In the middle part of the twentieth century, and especially after the Second World War, there was broad agreement that nation states were the most important membership organizations for human flourishing. Whether in the advanced industrial First World, the state socialist regimes or the post-colonial Third World countries, states took the lead in organizing societies as economies and political communities. In the liberal democratic 'welfare state' version, which was also offered as a model to developing countries, the legitimacy of these regimes was cast in terms of equality and justice. Welfare states were designed to cater for the free mobility of nationals within societies, conceived as systems for both economic and political membership, allowing entry to and exit from all internal organizations, but in ways that took account of their vulnerabilities and needs for protection.

States' schemes for redistribution and capacity building in this version saw these needs as arising within a class system based on industrial, capitalist production. They took little account of gender and 'race' as factors in oppression or exclusion within constituent membership systems.[10]

At the heart of these arrangements were compromises between organizations representing capital and ones representing labour, over sharing gains in productivity, which allowed expansion of productive capacities to be synchronized with demand for output.[11] Competition between firms in these regimes was typically oligopolistic,[12] and the state was empowered to manage employment and income distribution, by managing aggregate demand, by regulating growth in earnings, by transfers through social security schemes, and by the provision of public services. All this gave rise to monetary and fiscal regimes of permanent inflation, but this was managed and stabilized by means of international mechanisms of adjustment through exchange rates.

There were important variations in this model of states as membership systems between countries and regions, and a corresponding variation in versions of 'social citizenship'. In the UK, Canada, Australia and New Zealand, the central compromise relied on the bargaining power of trade unions in the leading sectors, and the rest of the system continued to be driven by the logic of markets. In

Japan (and, as they emerged, the newly industrialized countries of South-East Asia), the agenda was set by large firms, which shaped the regimes for labour markets and distribution as well as for production. In the Scandinavian countries, the trade unions, along with employers' organizations and the state, entered into more comprehensive arrangements over income transfers and public services, but left most productive decisions outside these, in the hands of private firms. And in the rest of Europe, the state played a leading role within all these spheres, through corporatist institutions with the other 'social partners', and there was more emphasis on social insurance transfers than public services, compared with the Scandinavian model.[13]

For the purposes of our analysis, it does not seem important to try to explain why these arrangements were less comprehensive, stable and enduring in the USA, or why corporations there and elsewhere started to break out of them in the late 1960s and early 1970s. Globalization began as a new strategy by firms for selling their products in world markets, leading to patterns of foreign direct investment, and thus to transnational rather than national oligopolies. Instead of relying on institutions for compromise with national labour forces to achieve productivity gains, these corporations depended on international finance capital to sustain their strategies within global markets.[14] The USA and (to a lesser extent) the UK were the bases for the main financial intermediaries and centres, and supported their interests. Through the International Monetary Fund and the World Bank, they pressed for deregulation of financial regimes, and this programme was gradually adopted by other First World countries.

This put financial institutions in control of economic policy and made all other institutions accountable to them. States' monetary and fiscal regimes became subject to evaluation by international financial markets. To pass these tests, governments had to control spending, keep taxes down and cut social protection. Market logics penetrated the institutions of employment and production, jobs and wages became the variables for adjustment. The whole hierarchy of factors that shaped the previous institutional system has been reversed, with governments courting international financial markets and transnational firms rather than national wage-earners and their organizations.

The stages of these transformations were by no means inevitable. We do not subscribe to the kind of economic determinism that sees political developments as always subordinate to economic interests. But once finance capital got in position to steer the deployment of productive capital, and corporations no longer relied on improving the productivity of First World labour forces, there was a dynamic between interdependent but competing states towards the adoption of market-driven institutions. This involved changing taxation rules in favour of mobile, international agents; making labour markets more 'flexible' by relaxing regulations in some sectors; privatizing public infrastructural assets and services; and increasing the proportion of pensions funded by individuals.[15] These shifts were embraced by governments in the Anglo-Saxon countries, and adopted piecemeal, with varying degrees of reluctance, by those which practised other variations. The intermediate and developing countries were often required to accept them as debt or fiscal crises forced them to borrow from international organizations.

Hence what started as a strategy for firms to sell the same products all over the world led to them making them everywhere, borrowing in all financial markets, recruiting staff without regard to nationality, and creating a global production and distribution process.[16] This allowed financial organizations worldwide to be integrated, a free trade agenda to be set, and the world economy to function as a whole system. The implications of all these transformations will be analysed in chapter 2.

This was the context in which the state socialist system of the Soviet Bloc countries collapsed, and their institutions were reconstructed under the guidance of the International Monetary Fund and the World Bank. It was also the context for the growth of migration from post-communist and developing states, and increased mobility within developed ones, as a response to crises and conflicts within an integrated world system. Mass movements across borders were part of a set of 'supply-side innovations' by losers in this system,[17] along with the huge shift back to subsistence production in the post-communist countries, and to informal economic activity more generally. Those who cannot any more look to national systems for their protection, those who lost out to more mobile and adaptable rivals, those displaced by international business incursions, and those forced out by the upsurge of armed conflicts all see movement across borders as one of their strategic options, and perhaps one of a number of simultaneous strategies pursued by members of their social units – families, kinship or communal networks. Migrants and poor people taking part in informal economic activity in turn become agents of transformation and targets for new forms of international regulation.

In the next section, we will consider in more detail how these transformations affected the nature of membership organizations, and the patterns of mobility between them. This requires us to analyse the shifting boundaries of both economic and political systems, and how the identities and interests of their members were reconstructed.

The nature of organizational boundaries

Theories of globalization tend to emphasize the processes through which economic agents transcended the restraints and boundaries of national political communities, and broke down the effectiveness of their systems for social citizenship. They also stress the role of international agencies, under the aegis of the US Treasury, in promoting programmes for the liberalization of capital markets, the deregulation of labour markets, the privatization of public services and the removal of barriers to free trade.[18] All this suggests that these were transformations that opened up previously enclosed, protected systems to market forces, aiming to achieve greater efficiency through the 'creative destruction' they accomplish.

But this is only half the story. Economic organizations like firms are themselves membership systems, with boundaries of their own. The virtues of markets in achieving efficient allocation through *competition* are only possible because such organizations are distinct from each other. Furthermore, globalization began with the transformation of firms, as collective physical assets and human skills, into enterprises which were transnational in their scope and scale.[19] The other side of the story of globalization is how such economic organizations were able to offer alternative membership systems to the ones supplied by states. Their capacities to subvert the political regulation of markets, states' provision of public services and governments' protection of their citizens all relied on their abilities to set new boundaries of new forms of membership.

The economic legitimacy of welfare states rested on governments' claims to be fair and rational arbiters, acting to correct 'market failures'. In the technical jargon of economic theory, these included the efficient provision of 'public goods', which market agents would always under-supply, because there was no means of excluding consumers unwilling to pay their full price, and because additional users did not decrease the benefit derived by the original consumers, and hence there was no 'rivalry' in consumption. The standard examples of these corrections for market failure cited in the economic literature since Adam Smith were law and order, defence and environmental protection, but this list had been extended to include the provision of infrastructural goods, compensations for externalities,[20] education and health care, and eventually also (by the 1950s and 1960s) redistribution through progressive taxation and social security schemes. One of the reasons why the programme of globalization has been so successful is that it has been able to cast doubt on whether governments are the best agencies for supplying these goods.

Part of this success has stemmed from new technologies and organizational capacities, which allow collective facilities to be provided to a limited number of people. Because it has become technically possible to create new boundaries, excluding non-members from the benefits of belonging, and making sure that members pay the full price for those they enjoy, these goods are transformed from 'public' to 'collective' goods, and firms can make profits from supplying them. Terms such as 'subscribers', 'contributors' and 'customers' are used for the members of these economic organizations. Furthermore, these membership systems are often international, so governments lose out in two ways: first, they can no longer sustain the claim that they are the only feasible provider; and, second, they cannot limit provision to national citizens.

The obvious example of such a process is telecommunications.[21] The first telephone networks were expensive and complex to create, and it made sense for national governments to bear the costs of establishing them, become monopoly suppliers of the service and make standard charges for installation and access. (National oligopolistic enterprises made handsome profits from manufacturing the equipment and laying down this infrastructure.) But technological innovations such as satellites and mobile phones have allowed the development of commercial networks, through which subscriber/members, by dialling codes or purchasing cards or instruments, can join a range of transnational systems with their own special charge rates and access facilities.

Education, health, social care and criminal corrections are now aspects of states' role that can be supplied through these new forms of organization. In the branch of economic theory known as 'fiscal federalism', they are called 'clubs', and the 'intermediate goods' they provide for their members are neither purely private nor purely public. Although the original model for these was a swimming pool,[22] surrounded by a fence and charging membership dues, such voluntary associations are no longer representative of either the organizations or the collective amenities they provide. Someone using a toll road, subscribing to a pay-to-view TV channel, attending a private hospital or school, or living in a private care home or prison would not necessarily think of him- or herself as a member of a club; but all these rely on similar systems of cost-sharing in their production, collective consumption and access through fees. The commercial firms that supply them either sell directly to subscribers, or have their membership funded by the public purse, under contracts with governments.

Furthermore, since each of these goods has different economic properties (in relation to the technologies of excluding non-members, and the sharing of costs among members), there is no reason why the same size and structure of 'clubs' should be optimal for each good,[23] or why they should recruit from the same overall population. This has very important implications for the boundaries of administrative authorities and political communities. Who should most efficiently be included as members in such organizations varies between goods and between populations. In the last resort, different optimum structures and sizes will be recommended, depending on whether the standpoint is that of the members of the organization, or the population as a whole, and whether the local, national or regional population is taken into account.[24]

In the phase of globalization that coincides with the start of this century, public infrastructures and public services (transport systems, postal services, health and social care, education and internal security) are particular targets for transformation, and new transnational corporations are being developed for profitable involvement in these processes. For national governments, which gained their legitimacy from providing a basic structure that was available to all, from creating common interests in improving public services, and from inclusive membership systems of sharing and redistribution for the sake of social justice, this creates many dilemmas. It also raises questions about the appropriate administrative boundaries for provision, and borders for states.

These issues are disputed among the four standpoints introduced at the start of this chapter. From a national perspective, the effectiveness of states for the protection of their citizens, and of public services in achieving this, is still paramount. But international organizations, and especially the World Trade Organization, are now committed to negotiations for a GATS, which will open up these services to competition, privatization and restructuring.[25] The arguments for these transformations are largely derived from the economic theory of fiscal federalism and clubs, but they are strongly resisted, from an ethical standpoint, by many NGOs, trade unions, professional and community groups.[26]

National governments face hard choices over these issues. Either they must try to fend off the incursions of transnational companies, in defence of their public services; or they must embrace the change, and try to gain advantage over competitor states by entering the field as predators rather than prey within this global regime. The UK government has chosen the latter option, preferring to build on privatizations and public–private partnerships already carried through by Conservative administrations, to steal a march on other First World countries, and gain a lucrative foothold in the market for transforming the infrastructures of the post-communist and developing worlds.[27] As in the USA, businesses specializing in education and health are being incubated,[28] in preparation for the global opportunities for strategic advantage under a revised GATS.[29]

Rattled by hostile campaigns against the Agreement by NGOs and anti-globalization movements, the World Trade Organization has emphasized that national governments will still retain the rights to regulate in pursuit of their objectives, and to decide which services to open to foreign suppliers, under what conditions.[30] But these decisions raise fundamental issues about the autonomy of nation states, and their powers to control their populations and their borders.

Sovereignty

So far, our analysis has dealt very little in issues of political power, or the differences in power between states. However, such questions are important in debates on globalization, and on the significance of migration. From a nationalist standpoint, state sovereignty should allow control over economic and social policy, including immigration rules. Globalists see the role of international organizations and market forces as more benign, but Washington Consensus gamekeeper-turned-poacher Joseph Stiglitz acknowledges that the IMF in particular has at times imposed regimes (such as the liberalization of capital markets) in the interests of the US Treasury and US finance capital. After the events of 11 September 2001, an alliance of the North American and European states justified using war as an instrument for 'regime change', and this has provoked strong ethical opposition from NGOs and churches.

> Sovereignty entails obligations. One is not to massacre your own people. Another is not to support terrorism in any way. If a government fails to meet these obligations, then it forfeits some of the normal advantages of sovereignty, including the right to be left alone inside your own territory. Other governments, including the US, gain the right to intervene. In the case of terrorism, this can lead to a right to preventive or peremptory [sic] self-defence.[31]

In an interview with the *New Yorker* in March 2002, Richard Haass, director of policy planning for the US Secretary of State, Colin Powell, used these words to describe a new doctrine of limited sovereignty developed in the USA and the UK in the wake of the attacks on the

Twin Towers and the Pentagon. 'State failure' was linked
with loss of control over migration, as well as drug trafficking and terrorism. In the same week, Robert Cooper, until
shortly before this one of Tony Blair's close foreign policy
advisers, argued for voluntary limitations of sovereignty
('co-operative empires') in a pamphlet called *Reordering
the World*.[32] Failed states, or specially vulnerable ones,
could subject themselves to forms of protection from
stronger others in a new version of an old idea,
imperialism.

During the earlier phases of globalization, it seemed
necessary – even for globalists – to try to buttress the idea
of national sovereignty, and to disguise its nature.[33] On
the one hand, international organizations recognized but
regulated states' autonomy. 'National government is
locked into an array of global, regional and multilateral
systems of governance' that 'delimit and curtail the principle of effective state power'.[34] On the other, the mobility
associated with economic interdependence meant states
were not separate, self-regulatory systems, but fluid,
porous and amorphous bodies. Nationalists attached particular significance to flows of population across borders.

The sinister side of such flows seemed to be confirmed
by the events of 11 September; yet confusingly (as far as
could be ascertained) the people who hijacked the airliners
and flew them into the buildings were not clandestine
entrants, but *legal* immigrants (students, technicians, professionals) of exactly the kind sought or recruited by First
World countries as of significant value to their economies.
Their action involved using instruments of transnational
communication against symbols of globalization and hege-
monic US power.

In the version of liberal democracy that seemed to have
triumphed by the end of the twentieth century, the principle of sovereignty provided the links between autonomy,

membership and governance. The basic units of liberal democratic theory are individual human beings, with equal status as autonomous moral agents.[35] Sovereignty links populations of such beings to territory and to collective rule by defining the political basis for membership. Democracy is rule by the people, but someone must first decide who 'the people' are.[36] 'Democratic decision making in any kind of association presupposes clearly defined boundaries of membership for the collective as a whole.'[37] On the other hand, the moral equality of persons implies that all are equally eligible for membership; but liberal democratic principles indicate that no rule for selecting between applicants (not even a lottery) should be imposed unless all have taken part in the decision to adopt this rule.[38] Neo-Hobbesian versions of states as independent sovereign entities cut through these problems; globalism, federalism and transnational ethics all tend to raise them.

Migration illustrates the precarious balance between the power of global and regional regimes and that of nation states. Freedom of movement for the purposes of business, study and tourism has become established throughout the world under rules sustained through international agreements. There is an international convention on rights to humanitarian protection for victims of war and oppression. But rules about who can work, who can settle and who can become a citizen are still the province of national governments. The tension between these three systems, existing side by side, is reflected in periodic 'moral panics' about immigration, asylum seeking, race relations and the cultural basis for political communities in First World countries.

In the politics of globalization, migration has become the focus for new regional regimes, which in turn intervene further afield to try to manage population flows.

Increasingly, these encourage short-term entry for the sake of flexible labour supply, but severely restrict long-term settlement. They block access to secondary movements of family members, so that those making a time-limited economic contribution through their jobs do not become long-term costs to taxpayers.

The European Union illustrates these processes. The creation of a single market with free movement for citizens of member states (but not for third-country nationals) in the Maastricht Treaty of 1991 was accompanied by new measures to strengthen external borders against migrants from post-communist Central and Eastern Europe, and asylum seekers from further afield (Fortress Europe).[39] But in 2000 the Commission proposed the widening of inward channels to meet specific shortages of skilled and unskilled workers.[40] At the same time, new measures against 'illegal immigrants'[41] and to deter asylum seekers were partly justified by increased opportunities for authorized entry through the expansion of those schemes. Management regimes involved extensive engagement with sending states, including police and migration control liaison.[42] These proposals emphasized concern to help sending countries achieve balanced economic development, the organizational links between the trafficking of people and international crime, and the potential benefits of managed recruitment for the economies of the host countries.

So the paradox of new migration management regimes is that national sovereignty in relation to border controls is shored up by supranational bodies like the EU; they also involve international organizations like the International Organization for Migration and the International Labour Office of the United Nations. Sovereignty must constantly make accommodations with globalist agencies and federalist institutions within this order, which perpetually engenders new intergovernmental links and co-operations, especially in the field of security.

Issues of power and enforcement are never very far from the surface of such engagements. Coercive power is evident in states' exclusions of unauthorized migrants, and in their restrictive containment or removal of asylum seekers. It is apparent in the relationships of strong, rich countries that receive migrants with poor, weak ones that send them. And it is obvious in the role of the USA, as global hegemon, in shaping international policies and interventions, which are justified by the supposed links between illegal immigration, drug trafficking, terrorism and government failure. The ethical issues raised by these uses of power, and their implications for equality and democracy, will be analysed in chapter 4.

Citizenship, mobility and social justice

The ethical critique of globalization focuses on its consequences, in terms of growing inequalities between individuals within political communities, and between states, and injustices in social and economic relations. A fundamental question raised by these criticisms is whether any set of institutions can transcend national citizenship as a basis for equality, justice and membership. Nationalist justifications of state sovereignty insist that this alone can achieve distributions according to these principles.[43] Globalists argue that their latest model for world economic development can reduce poverty and deliver the benefits of market integration to all.[44] Federalists claim that mobility can (under certain assumptions) provide new instruments for efficient and equitable allocation of collective goods, and some theorists of citizenship suggest that its rights and protections can be extended transnationally.[45]

As we saw in the previous section, the basic principle of liberalism, moral equality of all persons, and the basic principle for just governance in relations between members, democracy, both have difficulties over mobility between political communities. These are merely accentuated by globalization and accelerated movement of people across borders. So there are fundamental issues at stake in these ethical debates, including the legitimacy of the international order of nation states and the justification of global systems of governance.

In one sense, it seems straightforward to reconcile liberal versions of equality and justice with globalism. Justice requires impartial treatment: all individuals should be subject to the same set of social rules. Impartiality between individuals and neutrality about the good way of life implement the principle of moral equality. This version of justice is procedural and legal, and creates juridical equality. Hence it may be compatible with a great deal of inequality in the substantive sense. So the normative foundations of nationalist capitalism were not essentially different from those that international organizations strive to establish for the integrated global market. In the neoliberal (or libertarian) variant of this model,[46] individuals with juridically equal personal and property rights contract with each other for the supply of goods and services, with little normative purchase on the aggregate patterns of advantage and disadvantage, wealth and poverty, that these produce. The Washington Consensus programme of the 1980s and 1990s was inspired by this Nozickian vision; more recent models of world development and poverty reduction introduce Rawlsian restraints, for the sake of the least advantaged.

The claim that citizenship in the era of welfare states

provided something different from and more than this formal, procedural equality and justice therefore rests on the contents of their rules of allocation and the fairness of their outcomes. Instead of equal treatment, citizenship involved ideas of equality of resources or capabilities, and social justice was concerned with evaluating the distribution of access, rights and roles. It addressed more than the freedom of economic agents to conduct 'voluntary' exchanges; citizenship required autonomy, based on the facilities (such as income, education and health) to make real choices. Even if it turns out that these promises of social citizenship were only half-fulfilled, the concept provides standards of membership from which to evaluate the alternatives offered by globalism and federalism.

The contribution of globalist ideas to this debate lies in their insistence that the welfare of the world's population as a whole must be taken into account in any analysis of social justice. Whether or not the institutional model of their programmes goes anywhere near to achieving these standards, this principle is important, especially for the evaluation of migration rules.[47] In this sense, organizations like the World Bank do contribute to the search for a reconciliation between mobility and membership systems.

Federalist analyses are more ambitious. They set out a whole theory of distribution and membership, with the criteria for evaluating the organizational boundaries and structures of these for each collective good. One branch of this is concerned with the optimum relationship between levels of government;[48] another deals in how geographical mobility of individuals and households can lead to the optimum range of local jurisdictions.[49] Globalist and federalist political economy will be more fully introduced in chapter 2.

The central question is whether, in an integrated world

economy, any system of regulation can accomplish a coherent version of equality and justice. Can national citizenship be given sufficient transnational elements to protect the vulnerabilities of those who travel abroad, as well as those in greatest need who remain at home? Might international organizations gain the power to tax mobile capital (as in the Tobin tax proposal) for the sake of distributive equity? Could the new technological capacities of firms to exclude non-members from access to collective goods make political authorities redundant in some decisions about the allocation of resources? How might all these elements be balanced within a new model of global social justice? These issues will be tackled in the final chapter.

A central theme throughout the book will be the requirement, under conditions of globalization, to create stable relationships, for binding collective agreements, between footloose and rivalrous agents, and sedentary and vulnerable ones, with provision for those forced to flee persecution, and protection for those denied the choice to move. To say this is simply to restate the challenges laid down by Machiavelli and Hobbes at the dawn of the modern era.

The transformation of welfare states, and of social relationships generally, has largely been a consequence of differential mobility and access.[50] Money can be moved instantly across borders, businesses are transnational in scope, and people with skills are in demand in all countries. Hence states find it increasingly hard to tax mobile assets and people, and instead impose sales taxes and employment-related contributions. In terms of the liberal version of justice, political authorities are required to be neutral between mobile and immobile lifestyles, and to resolve conflicts of interest between nomadic and sedentary groups. This means that membership systems must provide resources in such a way as to allow mobility, but also support stability and interdependence.

Globalization has increased the scope for agents to improve their welfare through exit options, and reduced the effectiveness of voice and loyalty ones.[51] As A.O. Hirschman pointed out, market systems are mainly based on exit – leaving products, brands, firms, investment funds, pension schemes or whatever, in favour of ones offering greater individual advantage. Political institutions involve voice and loyalty, because members must believe that it is worth their while to participate in collective decisions, and to retain solidarity with fellow members.[52] Hirschman argued that all kinds of organizations – firms and NGOs as well as states – should try to balance exit, voice and loyalty, especially in the face of decline. Whatever membership systems evolve or are created in this century will face this challenge, and the fate of democracy as a principle of collective rule will depend on the achievement of this balance.

These systems will also have to provide for people with no material assets, few skills, bad health, disabilities or heavy responsibilities towards other family members, all over the world. At present, international organizations like the World Bank impose conditions on loans to poor countries, demanding that they give priority to the claims of these citizens; and First World states enforce conditions around benefits and services for these groups, requiring them to work and support each other. Financial dependence allows the exercise of power at each level, and puts those in need of assistance under the surveillance of vigilant authorities. We will investigate whether international credit and the resources for basic living can be supplied in ways that allow more autonomy for recipients.

Unlike workers recruited for their economic value, those who seek refuge from war, starvation or persecution encounter barriers as restrictive and deterrent as ever at the borders of the First World. Nowhere is this more vividly illustrated than in Australia, where asylum seekers are detained in remote camps, and have resorted to desperate measures, such as hunger strikes and sewing their lips together, to protest at their treatment. The protection of vulnerable migrants remains an unresolved problem for membership systems.

Conclusions

Although these issues have been presented through abstract perspectives on globalization, boundaries and membership, they affect every aspect of life. Not only choices about where to live and work, with whom to share risks, and to whom to pay dues and taxes, but also decisions about war, crime and security depend on the rules of these systems. Because they are all so closely related to each other, migration provides a useful focus for distinguishing between alternative approaches.

One day, any day, three migrants arrive in the UK from abroad. The first is a Kurdish teacher from Iraq, who comes concealed in the back of a lorry from France, applies for asylum soon after entering the country, and is admitted to a reception centre in a rural location. The second is a nurse from India, who goes straight to work at a nursing home in Sussex, where the company that employs her has already received her work permit, and will provide her with accommodation.[53] The third is a dentist from Poland, travelling with a coach party (all of whom say they are tourists) and carrying an invitation letter from a friend, staying in London. The day after moving into a shared room in this house, he starts work at a small textile factory in the north-east of the city, owned by a minority ethnic entrepreneur, for £2.25 an hour, well below the statutory minimum wage.[54]

In the past few years, the numbers entering the UK as asylum seekers have been around 70,000–80,000 per annum, those coming for employment under one of the several time-limited schemes for recruitment around 100,000, and the figures for irregular immigrants are unknown, possibly fewer than either of the other categories, possibly more. The occupational backgrounds of the three examples given are not unrepresentative. Most asylum seekers are educated and skilled;[55] the largest group of work permit holders are public service professionals;[56] and research on undocumented migrant workers suggests that these too have good qualifications and skills, though they typically do menial and low-paid work.[57]

So the human details of migration show the transformation that is taking place in societies, and particularly in public services. In postwar welfare states, these defined the substantial rights of membership and the common interests of citizens; they also provided the main content of policies over which political parties competed, the frameworks for civil interactions and the restraints on class conflicts. Under globalization, and specifically under GATS, staff of such systems are being dispersed across the world, and employed by privately owned or managed bodies, as the collective infrastructures of states are opened up for competition.

At the same time, UK citizens are moving abroad, for short or long stays. A salesman of defence equipment leaves for Pakistan in pursuit of a deal. Both National Health Service and private patients travel to Cape Town for heart operations and cancer treatments, in state and private hospitals.[58] A pensions expert goes to Russia, to advise the government about how to increase the proportion of contributions made by individuals. All these trips reflect boundary tensions and changes, the emergence of new cosmopolitan economic membership systems, and states' attempts to reconcile conflicts of interest between nomadic and sedentary populations.

Not all the losers of globalization remain sedentary. Some who are displaced by economic transformations and political upheavals move across borders, without meeting criteria for recruitment, or being able to pay the membership dues of economic organizations. The first half of this book analyses the political economy of mobility; the second part undertakes an ethical evaluation of the boundary rules of membership systems.

We aim to explain the relevance of organizational boundaries for issues of equality and justice. The four standpoints offer alternative analyses of the implications of global economic integration, none of which is complete or internally coherent. To overcome these problems, each must justify (or justify the abolition of) territorial borders and political memberships. The moral equality of persons is universal, so it demands that primary social goods are distributed globally, to the world's population as a whole. Both ethical and economic analyses point towards rights to income as the basis for equal autonomy, and to the basic income principle as the institutional means of distribution. Although the ethics of boundaries are logically distinct from such institutional questions, we treat them as interlinked themes for the new century.

2

The New Model of Global Governance

People crossing borders, like the examples just given, are helped or hindered by migration regimes. For some travellers, political boundaries are little more than markers, on journeys facilitated by governments. For others, they are barriers designed to keep out unwanted entrants. These rules form part of new systems of international regulation.

In what sense is the new world order an *order*? In the introductory chapter, we set out a framework for analysing the transformation of societies as systems of membership, and the role of mobility in these transformations. We introduced four perspectives on the integration of the world economy, and the significance of migration. In this chapter, we consider the contribution of two of them, globalism and federalism, to a new model of governance.

Globalism is primarily concerned with the relationships between markets and national governments. The International Monetary Fund is responsible for global financial stability; since the early 1980s, its officials have pursued a market-orientated programme for liberalization, deregulation and privatization worldwide. The World Bank makes loans to governments, and sets their conditions, in terms of restructuring financial institutions, labour markets and trade policies. The World Trade Organization governs international trade relations, and promotes free exchange of goods and services. The broad agreement on principles between these three international organizations and the US government during the final twenty years of the last century has been characterized as the Washington Consensus. Recently, however, the World Bank's responsibilities for economic development and the reduction of poverty have been the focus of some dissent by elements among its staff and advisers, and a change in emphasis in its policies.[1]

Globalism therefore addresses the transformative potential of markets for political institutions, and how new structures and policies can steer these for the benefit of the world's population. Mobility is a key factor in all markets, including labour markets; equilibrium is reached only because money, machines and people move to where they can be most productively deployed. But trade in products, between countries specializing in certain kinds of production, is an alternative to the migration of workers across national borders.[2] As a perspective on the economics of world development, the globalism of the international organizations favours free trade, rather than free movement of people. Hence globalism seldom challenges national governments in relation to restrictive immigration rules.

The theory of fiscal federalism is directly concerned with membership systems and their boundaries. It sees mobility between organizations of all kinds as a means by which agents express their choices over collective goods. In so far as local governments provide a range of such goods to their residents (for instance, an infrastructure of roads, drains, parks, libraries and sports facilities), federalists favour geographical mobility between jurisdictions as a way of achieving efficient allocations of public funds. In this sense, the mobility of people becomes as relevant an instrument of transformation as markets, and free movement is therefore an important principle of federalism.

At the level of policy, the theory suggests that many of the goods supplied by national governments might be more efficiently provided by firms, or by 'public–private partnerships' (as they are now known in the UK). Most of people's needs would therefore be met by a set of overlapping 'clubs' (in the sense defined on pp. 12–13), which might recruit members across territorial boundaries.[3] The best division of responsibilities between local, national and supranational political authorities, and the optimum size for each, would be reliant on the capacities of households to move in search of their preferred bundle of tax-funded goods.[4] Hence federalists recommend structures of governance (such as the EU) with several tiers, and rights of movement between member jurisdictions. Although this theory is seldom applied to the world as a whole, it tends to promote mobility across borders, and oppose migration restrictions.

These two perspectives are therefore different in their focus, and in their policy targets. But they tend to converge in the present phase of globalization, because this concerns the opening up of public infrastructures and government services to competition from economic organizations worldwide. Hence the programmes of liberalization, deregulation and privatization pursued by international organizations draw on ideas from the theory of federalism and economic clubs, and the transformations they aim to achieve involve the creation of new cosmopolitan membership systems, new kinds of political boundaries, new rules on mobility and new regimes of governance.

Our analysis will investigate the coherence of the new model that is emerging. In the first part of the chapter, we consider the significance of disagreements between the

IMF and the World Bank over 'market failure' and 'government failure', and of the Bank's new approaches on development and poverty. In particular, we explore whether globalists offer a clear view of the role of states in protecting their most vulnerable citizens, and the contribution of all membership systems (and of movement between them) to sharing the benefits of world economic integration.

In the second part, we turn to federalist accounts of the transformation of governance, and evaluate their claims to reconcile the provision of collective goods through exclusive membership systems with the collective power of political authority. In a global context, we explore whether the theory can prescribe institutions for the commercial supply of such goods that transcend political boundaries, and rules for mobility between territorial jurisdictions that are optimal for the whole world's population.

We argue that, despite the incoherences and contradictions within and between the two approaches we identify, they are being fused together in a new model of governance, which is global in its reach, but structured hierarchically to allow financial institutions to shape productive activities, and transnational corporations to gain access to supplies of labour and land. It provides a clear set of institutional designs, and sees democratic politics mainly as an obstacle to its purposes.

The model sets out the relationship between monetary systems, shareholders' property rights, fiscal regimes and public finance cultures, and gives private companies access to collective infrastructural provision. There are chains of accountability throughout this system, with the international organizations themselves at the top of its hierarchy. The structure determines the scope and limits of political authority within states, and hence the range of issues appropriate for popular sovereignty.

In the First World countries, these concern managing the transition to finance-dominated, knowledge-based economies, and creating appropriate systems for social reproduction. In the intermediate ones, they address the relations of production and patterns of distribution, but within strict externally determined parameters. In the developing, Third World countries, access to land, water, minerals and other natural resources shapes a harsher, often brutal politics of conflict over control of the state, and of access by foreign companies. Here the model makes national elites directly accountable to international organizations for the management of their most vulnerable communities (see pp. 41–7). But it also promotes market-based membership systems in which choices are expressed through 'exit' (changing employers, suppliers, clubs or locations), and narrows opportunities for effective 'voice' (participation, collective action), thus weakening 'loyalty' (solidarity, mutual protection).[5] This re-orientation makes movement across borders a more prominent strategic option, and requires systems for managing migration to be part of the overall scheme of global governance.[6]

All this transforms the nature and purposes of collective power, the processes through which it is constructed, and the forms taken by its exercise and implementation. To accommodate global financial institutions, production sites and product markets, states must provide for interactions between mobile economic agents and immobile local ones. This 'business-friendly environment', consisting of a juxtaposition of polarized attractive communities of choice, and deprived communities of fate, can demand the management of conflicts and contradictions, and an escalating use of force when these become unmanageable. In the developing world, such measures involve more violence and repression, as states seek to quell secessions, revolutions and defections, armed conflicts between groups over scarce resources, and the effects of natural crises and distress that constantly threaten human life itself.

Globalism in action

The IMF, the World Bank and the WTO were established after the Second World War, to sustain regimes of national economic regulation and welfare states (see p. 6). The rationale for international organizations was the need to provide financial stability and to correct failures of capital markets, so as to prevent crises in one country spreading to others. The assumptions behind their operations were that other forms of market failure (in sufficient aggregate demand to create full employment, in the supply of public goods, and in distributions for the sake of equity) would be dealt with by national governments. International organizations would help states achieve these objectives by their own efforts, including measures to balance exchange rates, capital flows and trade.

During the period of the Washington Consensus (roughly 1980–99), the aims of these organizations changed. They shifted their focus from market failure to government failure, and particularly to the inefficiencies and inequities of state regimes of economic management and welfare provision. Their new programme was derived from micro-economic analysis, and based on the transformative capacities of markets and competition, as universal forces for dynamism and growth. As conditions for monetary interventions and loans to governments, they demanded liberalization of capital markets, deregulation of labour markets and privatization of public services.

Even as the strategies of global banking companies and transnational businesses were creating an integrated world economy, they sought to open up state sectors to the forces of 'creative destruction'.

At the start of the new century, this consensus was seemingly shaken. In his book *Globalization and Its Discontents*, Joseph Stiglitz, a former Chairman of Advisers to the US Government, Chief Economist at the World Bank and Nobel Laureate in Economics (2001), strongly criticized the IMF's programme, echoing many of the campaigns by anti-globalization protesters, and the ethical objections of international NGOs.[7] While maintaining that economic integration could benefit all, he blamed the over-hasty implementation of one-size-fits-all measures, and especially capital market liberalization, for the impoverishment of the great mass of the world's population.[8] He also implicated the US Treasury in policies favouring financial market actors, including the enforcement of debt repayments, and accused the US government of hypocrisy in protecting its own industries and workers, but imposing open regimes on those of poorer countries.[9]

In this and the next section, we analyse whether globalism can itself provide a coherent alternative to the Washington Consensus model. The globalist perspective claims to be able to distinguish between market failure and government failure, and design institutions capable of delivering the advantages of an integrated world economy to the largest number of its inhabitants. We argue that there are theoretical holes in globalist analysis, and that attempts to balance development with poverty reduction remain unconvincing. Measures intended to empower and include the poor instead justify new accretions in the power of international organizations.

Postwar regimes of national economic regulation identified market organizations (especially capitalist corporations) as potential abusers of monopoly power and exploiters of unorganized labour. They aimed to create institutions for balancing these competing interests, and making them accountable to the public good. By contrast, the Washington Consensus saw politicians and bureaucrats as the main sources of abusive power and unjust distribution. It pointed to the very institutions of state regulation and welfare protection as the origins of such evils.

The common element in both these versions is the idea of 'rent-seeking'. In economic theory, 'rents' are the extra incomes that agents can accrue, above the amount that they would require to supply their services under competitive market conditions.[10] Hence the concept can be applied to capitalist firms, to labour unions, to politicians who accept bribes for allocating contracts, to bureaucrats who expand their budgets to oversupply public services, or even to government regimes which protect their national industries and labour forces by imposing tariffs. In all these examples, organizations act in members' interests to restrain competition among them, and gain economic advantage at the expense of unorganized others in their domain – smaller companies, consumers, non-unionized workers, taxpayers or foreigners.

But there are two difficulties about the ways in which this concept is deployed in globalist discourses, both those upholding and those criticizing the Washington Consensus. *All* organizations are *both* rent-seekers *and* forces for competition which break down coalitions built around rents. This is because all organizations are both membership systems for restraining competition and sharing costs,[11] and systems for mobilizing their members for competition with other organizations.[12] The same rules that specify mutual responsibilities and distribute collective benefits (in firms, trade unions, welfare schemes and political communities) also exclude outsiders and create advantages over them. But because all membership systems compete with each other (for resources and for members), they also erode the rents of other such systems, within the rules set by higher-level institutions.[13] So market-orientated organizations like firms and trade unions act to break down rent-seeking in political life, and government organizations act to break down rent-seeking among economic organizations.

Second, the need for interventions to correct 'market failure' grows with the prevalence of market institutions; but the opportunities for profitable activity by business increase where government has regulated, nationalized or provided in the public interest. So the nationalist systems of the postwar era (including the socialist regimes of the Soviet Bloc) were tempting targets for those financial and productive interests that could penetrate them under programmes for market transformations. The Washington Consensus, in targeting 'government failure', was necessarily opening protected enclaves to profit-motivated privatization. Furthermore, since the predatory organizations that were the instruments of programmes for liberalization were necessarily themselves rent-seekers, and the US government was itself a membership system for protection from market forces, it is naïve to be surprised that they both exploited these opportunities for their advantage.

This raises the question of whether international organizations like the IMF, World Bank and WTO could ever, under any set of assumptions, act as impartial, neutral regulators in the interests of the whole world's population. As a testing ground for this issue, the transformations of the Soviet Bloc countries and of China have provided huge-scale experiments in transitions from authoritarian central planning to markets and democracy. They also provide a focus for the disputes between the IMF and World Bank variants of globalism, as reported by Stiglitz. Central and Eastern Europe and the former Soviet Union were the sphere of influence of the IMF model, while the World Bank was the dominant interest in China.[14] The comparison provides revealing evidence of the shortcomings of both variants, and the uncriticized assumptions they share.

In Central and Eastern Europe and Russia, the transition programme recommended by the Washington Consensus was 'shock therapy'; it attempted to create institutions for channelling money to investments, for organizing resources for production, and for distributing products for consumption, which relied on private property, profits and prices. But it paid insufficient attention to the regulatory rules, norms and practices required to make a market system work effectively. Hence the combination of financial deregulation and the privatization of state assets resulted in asset-stripping by old-regime insiders, and the transfer of private funds abroad. As the productive economy collapsed, unemployment and poverty grew, crime soared and populations were left to their own informal devices. In Russia in 1998 this led to crises of the currency and the fiscal capabilities of government. The national incomes of Russia, the Ukraine and almost all the former Soviet republics are still lower than they were in 1989.[15]

Despite this, several economic commentators who are influential within the IMF count the Russian transformation as a success, and are critical of the more gradualist or pragmatic transitions of the Central and Eastern European (CEE) post-communist countries.[16] Such analyses claim that the latter states have been adopting institutions required for access to the European Union, which have led to high rates of unemployment (18 per cent in Poland

and 15 per cent in Slovakia in 2002), whereas Russia and the other CIS countries have benefited from focusing on structural reforms (their average unemployment rates are half those for the CEE states[17]). Forecasts for the higher growth of GDP in the former than the latter, only part of which can be attributed to their lower starting point,[18] are claimed to stem from lower income taxes, payroll taxes and social provision.[19] In particular, the CEE countries are criticized for not doing enough to activate claimants of unemployment benefits, or to make these systems more conditional with more pressures to claimants to be mobile, adaptable and willing to take low-paid short-term work. (Advocates of labour market flexibility argue that research shows unemployed people are keen to work, so 'any job is better than no job';[20] but if participation is more important than pay, productivity and performance, what exactly was wrong with state socialism, which claimed absolutely full – and compulsory – employment as its chief achievement?)

Such dilemmas do not afflict the Chinese government. It can be highly selective in how it introduces markets, because it retains absolute authority over the people and the ownership of most assets, especially land. It has therefore been able to develop certain areas, the Special Economic Zones, as export-orientated manufacturing bases for foreign direct investors, on the model of the South-East Asian 'tiger' economies.[21] In particular it has controlled mobility from its other provinces into these ones, and blocked it into Hong Kong, preserving the former British colony as a financial centre, providing capital for its industrialization programme.[22] In this way, the Chinese authorities, unaccountable to their populations, can pursue intentional policies of uneven development between regions, specializing in traditional and advanced methods of production, and in institutions for channelling global investment towards the latter.

It is interesting to read the comments of Stiglitz on his own role (along with Kenneth Arrow) as an adviser in these transformation processes in China.[23] In his account, the Chinese government resisted pressures by the US Treasury for liberalizing capital markets, or full-scale privatization, following the IMF model.[24] In line with his subsequent policy prescriptions for the World Bank, he counselled careful pacing and sequencing of reforms and restructurings, such as a two-tier price system and communal enterprise funds. Revealingly, he comments:

> Economic growth and development do not automatically confer personal freedom and civil rights. . . . There are cases of successful reforms done under dictatorship – Pinochet in Chile is one example. But the cases of dictatorships destroying their economies are even more common. . . . The outcomes in China were precisely the opposite of what the IMF would have predicted – but were totally consonant with what the gradualists had suggested, only better.[25]

This concedes that the main difference between the IMF and World Bank approaches was in the timing of reforms and restructurings, in retention of state control over the processes of implementation, and not in the ultimate goals of transformation. In recommending 'homegrown' institutional designs[26] and the retention of government control of the transition programme, Stiglitz endorses whatever kind of regime happens to hold power during these processes. The objection to dictatorship is its tendency towards rent-seeking corruption, not its unaccountability to citizens. Gradualist globalists are as positive towards market-orientated ultimate goals as are shock therapist globalists, and as indifferent to the principle of democratization.

The finished product of globalist transformation is a total system of governance of membership systems and markets, with accountability to financial markets, and ultimately to the IMF and the World Bank themselves. At its apex are regimes for exchange rates and 'optimal currency areas'. Developing countries are now advised to adopt floating rates or 'hard pegs', such as currency bonds or dollarization.[27] (This conclusion, drawn from crises in Latin America, East Asia and Russia in the 1990s, did not stave off the one in Argentina spreading to Uruguay and Brazil in 2002.) Common currencies may serve as instruments of fiscal discipline, as in the EU, where the Maastricht conditions reined in government borrowing and spending. What is less well known is that the post-communist EU candidate countries are being urged by the IMF to join the European Monetary Union, even before they achieve membership of the EU, to promote foreign direct investment, lower interest rates and improve competitiveness. Indeed one, Montenegro (though still formally part of the Yugoslav Federation), is already a member of the Euro Zone. Monetary policy leads politics.

The model for the post-communist and other intermediate economies prescribes an economic environment suitable for the growth of small businesses, as the most dynamic sector and the main sources of employment; the World Bank approves the pattern where over half of all employment and value added comes from enterprises with fewer than fifty workers.[28] In relation to privatization, corporate governance with strong protection for shareholders' property rights (against expropriation through state policies or management strategies) is strongly urged,[29] as if these former state-owned enterprises are the regional equivalents of the transnational corporations of the First World.

In reality, this recipe conceals a whole series of assumptions about the future role of post-communist and intermediate countries in the global economy, and specifically about their dependence upon and usefulness for the First World. After 1989, domestic markets for manufactured goods in the former communist countries were quickly captured by transnational corporations from the West, with the financial sector closely following, on the pattern already seen in Latin America. The far larger size of Western companies and banks was a key advantage, in terms of unit costs and financial power, and no enterprise in the transition states could hope to reach this scale; their best strategy was to integrate themselves into the production and supply chains of transnational corporations.[30] Small enterprises, of course, are even more disadvantaged and dependent in these regards, and need to find particular niches where quick adaptations and good relationships with local banks allow them to survive. The recommended model allows these countries to become profitable markets for transnational corporations, which can establish subsidiaries and branches run by local companies, and invest in large infrastructural projects such as energy and telecommunications. The designs for all other institutional features – law, public finance and labour markets – are derived from these inbuilt, economically imperialist assumptions.

It is no coincidence that this model gives rise to boundary problems that it cannot resolve. Mobility of the factors of production is fundamental to the neo-classical microeconomics on which the model is founded, and all political institutions are derived from micro-economics. In an integrated world economy, political communities make sense only in so far as they can be reconciled with these demands. Memberships are necessarily fluid and temporary because boundaries must allow the flows that optimize outcomes through markets. In an economic crisis, such as Russia's in 1998, or Argentina's in 2002, it is rational for the 'oligarchs' to want to move their money to foreign bank accounts, and the middle class to want to emigrate.[31] From a globalist perspective, it is unclear whether state borders are barriers to efficiency or institutions to be defended, or whether migration is a necessary safety-valve or a serious problem.

The governance of world poverty

However, two other dimensions of global governance are inescapable, and pose quite different problems for the international organizations that address these issues. The first is the fact that the huge majority of the world's landmass is still given over to the production of the means for subsistence, or of raw materials for industrial and agricultural production, or remains undeveloped yet necessary for reproducing the biological species of the planet. The second is that the vast majority of the world's human population remain extremely poor: in 2000, 1.2 billion out of the total 6 billion earned less than a dollar a day, and 2.8 billion less than 2 dollars a day.[32]

Since 11 September 2001, the links between poverty, resistance to world economic integration, and the governance of developing countries have become more apparent. Hence the new agendas of international organizations and the policies of First World states now strongly emphasize the connections between poverty alleviation, sustainable development and good governance. The global 'war against terrorism', and the overwhelming use of military force against 'failed' or 'rogue' states, are justified by appeals to a new programme for justice in the relationship between the rich countries and the poor ones.

The future of this programme relies on its capacity to transcend two earlier models of world development. The first, which informed the United Nations Declaration of

Human Rights, is still represented in nationalist and statist regimes like Saddam Hussein's Iraq and Robert Mugabe's Zimbabwe, and still finds some legitimation among its citizens in appeals to social rights and collective protection against the economic power of global market forces and transnational corporations. The second, embodied in the regimes that replaced such leaderships in most parts of Africa and Asia, appeals more to neo-liberal ideas of individual responsibilities, to property and civil rights, and to micro-economic fundamentals, and allows freer play to the activities and interests of global capitalism. But it has spawned its own versions of political corruption, public debt burdens, unsustainable technological change (such as GM crops) and environmental depredation. Neither the defiant resistance of the former, nor the compliant co-operation of the latter, has been enough to secure the mass of their populations from poverty; often the transition from the one to the other has involved civil wars, outside military interventions or political coups, and periods of increased immiseration. Above all, what is needed is a basis for a new kind of relationship between the organizations, enterprises and political authorities that control wealth in the First World, and those that preside over poor populations in the developing one.

The new model is therefore required to do something far more difficult than the prescription for monetary stability, fiscal prudence, institutional reform and labour-market flexibility reviewed in the previous section. First, because the issues at stake concern the productivity and the conservation of most of the Earth's landmass and its natural endowment, the model must reconcile agriculture and extraction with the stewardship of the environment. If the concerns of First World governance are increasingly about abstractions (like money) and invisibles (like services) – highly mobile and interchangeable between locations – those of the Third World are about assets and resources that are firmly rooted in territories. Hence forms of political authority that are concerned with rule over territory, and with access to physical and natural resources, are quite inescapable, and involve interactions between very large global actors and very small local producers, or subsistence survivors.

Second, because so many of these populations organize their social lives through units (kinship groups, communities, tribes) that are neither political (in the modern sense, involving complex administrative divisions between activities, legal distinctions over public and private spheres, and differentiated government functions) nor commercial (involving the selling of most products, or the purchasing of most resources), governance must connect this world of 'informal' interactions with those of capitalism and democracy. Since poverty is so closely linked to being peripheral to world markets and industrial production, since environmental threats are most obvious where economies are least developed, and since starvation and the mass movements of populations it provokes are endemic to such regions, the model must somehow show how governance can provide orderly relationships between these systems.

The new model (as set out, for example, in the World Bank's *World Development Report*[33]) does attempt to connect all these elements with 'good governance', albeit in a clumsy and unconvincing way. The long-term goal of economic development is still defined in the same terms as in the previous two decades – growth through market liberalization – but it is recognized that, in order to reduce vulnerability to natural disasters, achieve environmental sustainability, restrain the despoliation of forests and predation of rare species, and include indigenous rural populations in the whole process of managed change, new

institutions and new thinking are required. The key con-
cepts in the new model are 'opportunity', 'empowerment'
and 'security', and the goal is to help poor people develop
their assets, and increase the reliable returns on these.[34]

However, there is no coherence in the way in which
various discourses of collective action, social protection
and membership systems are combined in this institutional design. The central issue for globalism identified at
the start of this chapter – how the transformative potential
of world markets can be balanced by the organized power
of groups in ways that are efficient and equitable for all –
is only half-recognized and only indirectly addressed. The
Report's prescriptions, like the recommendations of Stiglitz's book, are a mishmash of regulatory, protective and
redistributive measures, some global (through the IMF
and the Bank itself), some national (in the Keynesian-
corporatist tradition), some local, traditional and communal. They serve to slow down transformations and allow
adjustments, rather than reverse or radically direct them.

States in the developing world are required to deliver a
version of this package under a kind of 'social contract'
with all their citizens.[35] But this is to be supplied not by
an all-powerful state, or through authoritarian control and
compulsion, but by negotiation and agreement between
civil-society organizations and market ones, by public–
private partnerships, and more at a local than a national
level. 'Sound governance, competition, and markets – and
free entry for multiple agents, whether government, non-
government or private – are essential for effective service
delivery, especially to poor people.'[36] Although the central
state is still responsible for the overall institutional framework for social provision and inclusion, the implementation of the model, and its adaptation to the needs of
diverse populations, is devolved under arrangements in
which NGOs, both international and indigenous, play a

far more important role. The state provides an overall enabling environment, monitoring and regulating the emergence of such local decentralized systems.[37]

In this, the World Bank is strongly influenced by theories of community and social capital that became fashionable in the 1990s.[38] According to these, poor people are disadvantaged as much by their lack of norms, rules and practices that are shared with more successful groups, and are favourable for economic success and political inclusion, as by their lack of resources. Because their strategies are orientated towards subsistence and survival, they do not participate in wider networks that might give access to advantage, both through market exchanges and in public policy. The task of NGOs is therefore significantly concerned with social capital building, 'to enhance their potential by linking them to intermediary organizations, broader markets, and public institutions'.[39] Although much of the analysis in terms of social capital is vague, the ultimate goal is 'increasing the capacity of poor people and the socially disadvantaged to engage society's power structure and articulate their interests and aspirations'.[40]

Hence, the World Bank's analysis and strategy is concerned to 'empower' poor people, both at the community level and through institutions that 'bridge' and 'link' between their networks and those of business and administration, with the NGO sector in a crucial role. 'Since poor people usually organize at the local level', in order to allow their voices to be heard in government, and enable local corporatist arrangements between interest groups to be built, 'actions will also be needed to strengthen their capacity to influence policy at the state and national levels, such as by linking local organizations to wider organizations'.[41]

The biggest doubt about the coherence and adequacy of the model as a vehicle for the alleviation of poverty is

how the constituent parts are supposed to mesh together
to produce this outcome. The programme maintains con-
tinuity with the neo-liberal theme of market reforms, but
with the goals of 'making markets work better for poor
people'.[42] Through fiscal devolution and the creation of
an appropriate legal and administrative environment, the
government should supervise the local supply of adequate
collective provision. Although the redistribution of land
(from large traditional owners to smaller, more productive
and commercially orientated ones) and other redistributions are emphasized, so are the limits of state action. 'In
today's globally integrated world intrusive state action can
undercut the functioning of markets and the incentives for
private investment, killing job opportunities, not creating
them.'[43] Problems over conflicts of interest between rich
and poor, and the differentials in power between them,
are acknowledged, but not resolved. Nor is it clear how
'support networks of poor people' can balance the market
power of transnational corporations in search of either raw
materials or primary products.

Equally unresolved is the issue of how the building of
communities and social capital can counter the strongest
dynamic in developing countries – the pull away from
poor rural areas towards large cities, and the creation of
impoverished shanty towns around their margins. Even a
successful strategy for the empowerment of poor people
at the local level that included them more effectively in
the networks through which membership and collective
action are sustained would be unlikely to offset movements of population towards conurbations, which has
been characteristic of this stage of development in all
societies, and has contributed to inequality, exploitation
and conflict. Nor would it be likely on its own to stem
migration towards the richer societies of the First and
Second Worlds.

In the next section, we show why the new model finds it difficult to address these issues directly, and why it therefore fails to offer a convincing programme for the governance of poor countries, or the alleviation of poverty in rich ones.

Public choice, membership and institutional design

The distinctive contribution of federalist perspectives is their recognition of the importance of membership systems. They aim to provide a coherent analysis of organizations of this kind, including political communities, and of movement between them. Hence they address exactly the issues that are overlooked or fudged by globalist approaches. They also concern themselves with the sectors of national economies – public infrastructures and services – that are the targets of the current phase of globalization. So they are highly relevant, at least in their theoretical insights, for our attempt to clarify the significance of mobility and migration in the political economy of the new century.

Federalism recognizes that these dilemmas are inescapable, for one simple reason. However mobile money, technology and people may be, one factor of production – land – is immobile. It supplies the basis for residence and physical interactions, as well as productive activity. So all economic choices involve decisions about how to develop specific areas of land, and all political choices include issues about how to govern territory, and in what sized units.

The new century has started with a ferment of competing ideas about these issues. This reflects the global mobility of business elites and economic organizations, the immobility of mass populations in traditional social infrastructures, and the transformation of political institutions. New economic conditions replicate aspects of those of the late medieval period,[44] as well as some of the nineteenth century; transport, trade and communications are growing faster than production itself, so that it is those involved in new, long-distance transactions who drive innovations over jurisdictions and infrastructures, because their requirements are often quite different from those of less mobile populations.

In Europe in the late medieval era, the demands of merchants, manufacturers and craftsmen led to the creation of free city states, with considerable autonomy from the sprawling empires that encompassed them.[45] In the nineteenth century, economic agents combined with administrators and soldiers to establish colonial rule. Both regimes rested on the creation of 'parallel worlds' – systems of governance for the dynamic, expansive, transnational sectors of economic activity that were functionally separate from those ruling indigenous, traditional, territorial ones. What seems again to be at stake is how to design political institutions for two-speed economies, with very different requirements, and how to create suitable environments for the people who will operate them.

Between these eras of radical political transformation, nation states became established, first in Europe, and then throughout the world, as the authorities best able to integrate their subjects into unified systems of governance, and mobilize them in competition with other states. They recognized each other through international treaties, and – towards the end of the last century – became the units of a world system.

What lie behind new globalist blueprints are economic forces, probing weaknesses in existing political structures, and selecting those that best fit newly emerging conditions. Debates in economic theory about 'the political economy of federalism'[46] or the 'analytical foundations of a fiscal constitution'[47] self-consciously echo the disputes between seventeenth-century philosophers over the rights of sovereigns,[48] between eighteenth-century constitutionalists over the virtues and defects of 'compound' or 'confederal' republics,[49] and between nineteenth-century jurists over the division of powers.[50]

As already noted (see p. 34), the model seeks to control rent-seeking by politicians and bureaucrats,[51] and to limit potential monopoly power of central government agents, and their 'Leviathan' extraction of maximum tax revenues, by decentralizing fiscal instruments. According to this view, the overall size of the public sector should be smaller, the greater the extent to which taxes and expenditures are decentralized.[52] Furthermore, although central government should have basic responsibility for macroeconomic stabilization and income redistribution, the provision of all other public services should be located at the lowest level of government encompassing (territorially) the relevant benefits and costs.[53] In other words, there will always be welfare gains from devolving responsibility for collective provision to local authorities, which can tailor output to the particular preferences and needs of their constituencies.

On the face of it, these theoretical assumptions and models give rise to a simple prescription – 'fiscal federalism'[54] (as it is known in the USA), or 'the principle of subsidiarity'[55] (as it is called in the European tradition). This version has already been very influential, especially in the UK, where budgets for public services have been devolved to local units (even though fiscal powers have not) under both Conservative and New Labour administrations. However, there are far more ambiguities in the conclusions that can be derived from these assumptions than at first are apparent, especially when the model attempts to prescribe for interactions between highly mobile agents and immobile ones, or to deal with public goods such as environmental protection. Hence we can recognize the emergence of a number of different sets of institutions, existing in parallel with each other, and responding to different sets of economic costs and benefits in a complex way. Above all, the theory reveals an ambiguity about the concept of *membership*, and the extent to which individuals can engage with or disengage from each other in different dimensions at the same time.

The first dimension concerns *political* membership – participation, collective action, civic qualities and virtues, and the respect for human rights. Historically, these considerations have provided arguments for small political units, and specifically for city states, in the work of the civic republican tradition of Plato, Aristotle, Rousseau and Montesquieu.[56] Translated into the present-day economic terminology of public choice theory, these advantages stem from the low costs of bargaining and reaching agreements between effective representatives of groups with transparent interests and political agendas.[57] Such ideas can be reframed (for instance, in terms of social capital theory) to justify devolution of power for the sake of the potential benefits for citizenship, involvement and social inclusion.[58] Here membership is active, it promotes self-rule and commitment to the common good, and institutions reflect common interests in agreements between groups with divergent particular interests.

However, such a model conceals difficult problems about the larger political authorities in which such units are embedded. In order to make them highly accountable to their citizens, constituent 'city states' must have considerable sovereignty, making the proper form of the larger authority a confederacy, and giving the confederate states rights of secession and veto over central government decisions.[59] The latter's focus should be on the integrity of its 'city states', and on control of interstate 'spillovers', costs associated with trade and migration between them for which they would otherwise not be required to pay compensation. In reality, only Switzerland (with six hundred years of practice) has proved able to sustain anything like such arrangements. Hence the pure model of political devolution cannot apply; arguments for the empowerment of local interest groups, and individual citizens, must rest on the more general grounds of giving them greater stakes in participation, and in the outcomes of local bargaining agreements.

The second dimension is the *economic* membership of sharing in the costs of providing collective goods – infrastructural amenities and services – that sustain both business activity and personal consumption. Here the key questions concern the most efficient provision of the optimum supply of such goods, and give rise to very different arguments for devolution, and very different kinds of local authorities. Although there is an independent case to be made in terms of 'local and particular' public goods (corresponding to the territory in which the sum of residents' marginal benefits equals marginal cost),[60] this approach is strongly associated with the work of Charles Tiebout on intergovernmental competition[61] – small cities competing for highly mobile residents as an institutional way of ensuring efficiency in public finance and administration. The Tiebout model makes a number of unrealistic assumptions: of excludable collective goods produced with contestable technologies: costless mobility of perfectly informed households between a potentially infinite number of jurisdictions, each with the capacity to produce the most attractive features of its competitors, and no jurisdictional externalities. However, this version of the basis for devolved responsibilities has been extremely influential, because it promises ways in which informed and mobile citizens can discipline public-service providers, simply by moving to more efficient local authorities, and suggests that, for every level of output of a collective good 'there is a technically-efficient population size that minimizes the average cost per household of providing that service'.[62]

Thus, whereas for *political* membership the optimum form involves stable groups with trusted representatives and clearcut interests, leading to durable institutions and reliable bargains with other, similar groupings, for *economic* memberships that share costs of efficiently supplied collective goods the form is fluid, temporary and contingent on the particularities of the good in question, and the availability of attractive options elsewhere. Voting with the feet becomes the public choice equivalent to market consumption,[63] and welfare gains from decentralization stem from sorting populations into like groups, in terms of their preferences over public goods and their abilities to pay for them. Obviously this means that rich people will tend to be segregated from poor, and the least mobile will be concentrated in jurisdictions with the worst infrastructures.[64]

Furthermore, the arguments for more fluid and provisional governance systems, competing with each other for mobile memberships and mobile resources, are strongly reinforced by arguments over the institutional environments that most favour economic growth. Several theorists argue that the fiscal competition between local authorities on the Tiebout model limits taxation of income and capital, enhancing investment and economic development.[65] This is partly because such authorities face 'hard budget constraints' (they cannot create their own money, or access unlimited credit), and partly because of the potential exit of these sources of revenue.[66] The latter applies particularly to taxes used for redistributive transfers, from which rich, mobile members gain no benefit; hence tax burdens shift from mobile resources to fixed ones, and from redistributive systems to ones that tax the advantages that users get from infrastructural facilities and collective services.[67] This is a clear example of the power associated with greater mobility shaping the design of systems of governance.

Taken together, the requirements of decentralization for the sake of political participation, citizenship and democracy therefore point to very different institutional designs from those for the efficient supply of public goods.[68] But these contradictions can be partly reconciled through the role of central government, and by separating membership of political authorities from membership of the systems through which public services are provided. In this way, politics comes to be concerned with a range of issues over public order, property and personal rights, and the overall regulation of the public sphere, while the supply of collective infrastructural goods and services becomes the province of a very different kind of decision making, whose main concerns are economic efficiency. This allows an accommodation of sorts between the interests of highly mobile agents, in pursuit of rapid transformation and development, and immobile local populations, attempting to sustain their ways of life. The forms taken by these accommodations in the First World, the post-communist countries and the developing economies are, of course, extremely varied.

The role of the central state is required to adapt to this new division in dimensions of membership, and the structures through which decisions are taken. Some forms of public provision are likely to be consistently undersupplied under decentralizing regimes, notably environmental protection[69] and poverty alleviation, both of which become victims of a 'race to the bottom' through tax competition between smaller local authorities.[70] In order to counteract this, central government becomes more involved in raising taxes for income transfers, and in environmental regulation. Furthermore, it uses intergovernmental grants and revenue sharing (redistributing its own revenues to local authorities) to offset the fragmenting effects of decentralization. Social cohesion, risk equalization and balanced development all demand transfers from central authorities to regional or local ones, to alleviate tensions between political and economic dimensions of membership, or to allow the advantages of both to be gained. Thus, for instance, the German Federal government uses large grants to its constituent *Länder* for these purposes,[71] while the UK government raises most revenue for public services, but transfers it to the smallest possible spending units (such as primary health care trusts, schools and local 'partnerships') under complex initiatives, zones and formulae, related to needs and performances.

Furthermore, for federalists there are not two but three sets of principles at work here. For some goods, the optimum membership system may take the form of a functional 'club', recruiting across local government boundaries, or even across state borders (see pp. 10–14). For others (and especially those relating to physical infrastructures), populations are best divided between territorial jurisdictions, each providing a bundle of goods, with households voting with their feet between them. Hence membership systems overlap in complex ways, but both clubs and territorial jurisdictions tend to segregate populations according to their incomes and tastes. In both clubs and districts, efficiency is achieved by sorting members according to the quality of goods they require, and the contributions (or local taxes) they can afford to pay. It is left to the central authority to ensure democratic accountability at all levels, to co-ordinate the decisions of each, and supply equity in overall distribution of resources. But who or what is to determine the membership of this national political community itself?

One major paradox is that economic membership takes no account of citizenship or nationality: like globalization itself, it sees national boundaries as potential barriers to efficiency, and encourages movements of resources for the production of collective goods and services (including staff) to flow freely in pursuit of the most cost-effective allocations. Yet the agenda of empowerment through political decentralization can only embrace immobile or less mobile populations if it allows them some control over collective decisions, and offsets the economic power of mobile interests. This helps to explain why immigration has risen to the top of the political agendas of First World countries, as immobile citizens protest about distributive outcomes that leave them poor and excluded, and demand that national and local political authorities take collective action to defend their interests against those mobile agents. In this situation, settled immigrants (often poorer than those who protest about their presence and their access to collective resources) serve as proxy targets for the subversion of systems of social protection that have been swept away by global market forces, through the programmes of international regimes.

Conclusions

The globalist perspective on world development highlights the benefits of mobility through markets. Impoverished peasants in developing countries leave their farms to work in factories owned by transnational corporations. The savings of workers in First World states are channelled,

through banks and pension funds, to finance these investments. New technologies replace traditional methods,
incomes rise, health standards and quality of life improve.
The products made in developing countries supply
cheaper goods for consumers in developed ones, and
everyone is better off. The integration of the world economy allows the whole system to be managed, to optimize
global welfare. Crises and volatilities, threatening peasants' livelihoods, workers' wages, savers' pensions and
entrepreneurs' investments, signal the need for reforms in
systems of governance, which can ultimately give stable,
sustainable growth.

But these systems form a hierarchical order, making all
political authorities accountable to financial markets and
– in the case of the debt-laden developing countries – to
the international financial agencies, as global regulators.
The joint IMF/World Bank International Development
Association refers to the Poverty Reduction Strategy
Papers it requires from such countries as their 'business
plans',[72] and demands that these include evidence of
'integrity and transparency of public expenditure management and procurement systems'[73] and their 'social, structural and key sectoral policies, which covers the policy
reform and institutional development priorities',[74] in order
to assess applications for assistance. In other words, the
model allows such agencies to integrate these countries,
including their most remote communities, into the systems of accountability of the new global order.

Those who sit at the apex of this order acknowledge
that it is still a system for 'divergence and worldwide
income inequality'.[75] Despite the new emphasis on poverty reduction, the most marked feature of the integration
of the world economy has been 'the widening gap in
average incomes between the richest and the poorest
countries. In 1960 per capita GDP in the richest 20

countries was 18 times that in the poorest 20 countries. By 1995 this gap had widened to 37 times, a phenomenon often referred to as *divergence*.'[76]

Within states, the picture on inequality is less clear. Some have moved spectacularly in the direction of greater inequalities, especially the post-communist countries of the former USSR, and of Eastern Europe, where the introduction of private ownership and markets has reduced around 90 per cent of the population to the income levels previously experienced by the poorest 10 per cent, but a well-placed elite has become very wealthy. Among the First World countries, those which come closest to the new model of governance (the USA, the UK and New Zealand) are also the ones where inequalities have grown fastest. Among the rest of the world's states, inequalities have increased in some (such as China, Mexico and Bangladesh[77]), but reduced in others (such as Brazil[78]). Growth has contributed more to inequality than to poverty reduction in some, but both have occurred simultaneously in India.[79]

Federalism recognizes that these are political issues as well as economic ones, and that any model of governance deals in systems of membership and the political boundaries of territories. It presents a more sophisticated method of analysing the issues raised by globalism, explaining how economic 'clubs' can meet many of the needs previously supplied by local and national governments, and how they can recruit members across political borders (see pp. 13–14). It also shows how the development of land relates the provision of infrastructural facilities to the mobility of people, and how this in turn gives rise to a theory of territorial division and political membership. All this has influenced both international organizations (especially the WTO) and national governments in the transformation of governance. Globalist and federalist ideas converge in GATS. But fiscal federalism, the theory of overlapping transnational clubs and the dynamics of voting with the feet cannot – either separately or collectively – prescribe a global model of membership systems. This is because the optimum size and structure of each system cannot be specified without first identifying the populations eligible for membership, but the population available for selection depends in turn upon political boundaries.[80]

Meanwhile, migration management regimes have become key features of global governance systems, as 'turbo-capitalism'[81] generates winners and losers from its creative destruction. The integration of the productive economy requires mobility of managers and workers across borders; the transformation of public services now demands mobility of staff and service users also. Migration regimes facilitate such movements. But growing inequalities between rich and poor countries, political conflicts and financial crises all stimulate movements across borders. In the next chapter, we show how migration patterns reflect adaptation to these transformations as migrants develop new economic improvizations, new lifestyles and new social relationships.

3

The Political Economy of Migration

Migration is controversial. Nationalists argue that states have the right to recruit or restrict according to the interests of their citizens, and to select applicants for entry. Globalists prescribe international migration management regimes to regulate population flows across borders, in pursuit of sustainable growth and the welfare of all. International organizations also recognize the need for humanitarian protection to provide for the breakdown of the political order (wars and internal conflicts).

Federalists, as we have seen, draw attention to difficult issues in the political economy of migration. The economics of infrastructural provision for land may prescribe uneven development of territory, both within and between states. For different collective goods, optimum size and structure of administrative units varies, and the best results may require transnational selection. So mobility is a precondition for sorting populations into districts with efficient supplies of local public goods, and migration (or short-term movements across borders for staff and service users) may be desirable for optimal provision to meet other social needs. Migration regimes must allow for overlapping jurisdictions.

Critics of globalization draw attention to these anomalies. But campaigners also denounce the excesses of nationalism, and the evils of its racist versions. Ethical critiques and protests focus on victims of globalism and nationalism (poor migrants and refugees) in their evaluations of management systems.

During the era of national economic regulation, European states had large fluctuations in migration, and shifts in migration policies. The twenty years after the Second World War saw huge movements of population, some for economic and some for political reasons. On the one hand, northern European economies recruited mainly unskilled workers from the Mediterranean region and (in the case of the UK) from further afield. On the other, millions fled the communist regimes established in Central and Eastern Europe and in China, and millions more relocated to leave or join the newly independent polities of the developing world – 14 million crossed the border between India and Pakistan on partition in 1947[1] – or to return from former colonies.

Other massive migratory flows have comprised both these elements. The exodus of populations from Europe to North America and Australasia in the second half of the nineteenth century was proportionately larger than any movement in the twentieth.[2] These flows, for the sake of both economic opportunity and political freedom, were welcomed as congruent with the transnational political economy of the major powers in that period (movements of capital and the opening up of markets). But when migratory pressures from China and India built up in the twenty years before the First World War, all these same states erected barriers against such immigration.[3]

Our analysis in the previous chapters suggests that the present-day political economy of globalization demands new channels for the movement of financial, managerial and technical elites, and a range of highly skilled workers. We call these 'global nomads', because they often move from country to country. Strictly speaking, nomads are supposed to take all their property with them, and move as clans or tribes. Some global nomads do move lock, stock and barrel, and take their households with them (see pp. 84–5); others move alone.

At the same time, other populations all over the world flee or choose to move across borders for a mixture of political and economic reasons, either for safety, or as part of strategies to gain advantages from transnational activity and membership. Some of these, too, are nomadic, and keep moving on, either as asylum seekers, or as irregular migrants, supporting themselves in shadow economies.

Migration management regimes attempt to regulate these processes. As economic membership systems – from firms and clubs to communal subsistence and support networks – become more transnational, societies become more diverse and fluid, and political membership (with its rights and duties) more problematic.

National populations must respond to new conditions, set by international organizations and global market forces. Substantial rights to resources, provided by states, become less reliable, and 'supply-side' adaptations essential. Earlier waves of migrants find themselves disadvantaged in competition that demands employability, enterprise and mobility. Often they were among the first to be redundant as industrial employment contracted, and their offspring have least access to advantageous education and training for the expanding financial, professional and service sectors. They are forced to rely on informal improvizations and survival strategies. Like large groups of indigenous losers, they become isolated from mainstream social systems and resources; but they are then blamed, and perceived as rivals by native outsiders. Even their rights to be part of the society are questioned.[4]

In this way, 'immigration' comes to be a term that

connotes all the unresolved issues of membership in present-day societies. It mobilizes the resentment of those
made insecure by their vulnerability to global competition;
it taps into rivalries between excluded groups; it links the
fate of immobile and impoverished ethnic minority communities with the threat of mobile and resourceful newcomers, seen as further subverting the protections of
citizenship. It allows the politics of nationalism and 'race'
to be rekindled, and exposes the fragility of liberal democratic institutions.

The purpose of this chapter is to distinguish between
the different elements in current cross-border movements
of population. It is also to show that migration is not a
single phenomenon, with one central 'essence' and causal
explanation. There are as many kinds of migration as
there are ways of life that are sedentary, and migrants are
as varied in their characteristics, motives and behaviours
as sedentary people. What migrants do, like anyone else,
is adapt their strategies to the opportunities and constraints (including transport costs, entry conditions and
access to long-term settlement) of their wider institutional
environment. If there is a generalizable difference between
migrants and non-migrants, it is that the former are
probably more travel-tolerant and less risk-averse, and
that the latter rely more on location-specific insider advantages.[5] Hence migrants have a wider choice of strategies
than non-migrants, but sacrifice the advantages gained
from local systems of membership. They also rely more
on informal systems, including friendship groups, community and faith-based associations.

Migration pathways are not random; they usually follow
historical (such as colonial) links and economic connections.[6] Flows of people from particular countries in the
developing world take the reverse route of flows of capital
from specific developed countries.[7] Migration heads

especially towards global cities, where there is a seemingly insatiable demand for low-wage service workers, as well as high-salary financial, managerial, technical and professional recruits.[8] Migration is not directly related to population growth, or to poverty or conflict, except in the immediate aftermath of wars and famines. Migrants travel to join established groups of settlers, who provide bridgeheads and transitional arrangements for them in receiving countries.[9] But they also retain links with their countries of origin, and with chains of other migrants, distributed through intervening states.[10] In this sense, migration is not an isolated decision, pursued by an individual agent, but a kind of collective action,[11] involving families, kinship groups and often also communal resources, and therefore requiring a certain kind of social capital.

The model for global transformation set out in the previous chapter demands open channels for transnational business, for study and tourism, and for the recruitment of suitable staff, in an integrated world market. This stimulates forms of transnational enterprise in developing countries, reverse movements in micro-capitalist ventures,[12] or niches of ethnic production in First World countries.[13] Asylum seeking and irregular migration are triggered by political and economic upheavals in the wake of this transformation.[14] States both accommodate new flows required by economic integration, and restrict movement caused by its impact.

This chapter analyses migration as a requirement of, a response to and a resistance against, global institutional transformations and the integration of the world economy. By clarifying all these dimensions of migration, it prepares the ground for the analysis of population flows as challenges to the principles of political membership.

The extent of population movements

The first question for this analysis is whether there is a 'world migration crisis', as some have claimed.[15] Do current cross-border population movements threaten the model for global transformation laid down by international organizations more than they achieve its purposes? Does their challenge to states and their versions of political membership destabilize the new world order of economic integration, or push forward its agendas for adaptation and change?

Border crossings for business and tourism have grown exponentially in the past quarter-century, but movements for settlement have not come near levels of earlier periods of migration. Whether measured in terms of flows or proportions of people living outside their countries of citizenship, current rates are rather modest. Even asylum seeking, which grew most rapidly from the late 1980s (especially in the wake of the collapse of the Soviet Union and its satellite regimes), peaked around 1993, when there were some 19 million refugees worldwide.[16] By 2002 this had fallen to about 12 million.[17]

Most migrants living and working abroad are found in developing countries. In 2000, there were 34 million who had lived outside their country of citizenship for more than a year in sub-Saharan Africa, and 51 million in Asia, out of a world total of 100 million.[18] Among the far smaller number of the world's refugees, again the vast majority come from Africa and Asia, and are living in states adjacent to the ones they have fled (9 million out of 12 million).[19] The former Yugoslavia and Palestine are the only ones from outside Asia and Africa to figure in the top twenty countries from which the world's refugees have fled.[20]

Proportions of national populations leaving their homelands are far smaller than during previous migrations.
During the whole nineteenth century, more than 18 million people emigrated from the British Isles, while the
home population grew by 31 million.[21] In other words,
over a third of the natural increase went abroad. Similarly,
in Europe as a whole, nearly 40 per cent of the growth in
population was offset by emigration in some decades of
that century.[22] By comparison, the increase in the population of all Third World countries in the 1980s was an
average of 90 million a year, of whom only 3 to 4 million
emigrated, an average of less than 4 per cent.[23] This was
also a far lower rate than the immigrations from Mediterranean countries to northern Europe in the 1960s and
1970s, or from the Caribbean states to the USA up to the
1980s. Migrant workers represented 19.5 per cent of
national labour forces in Algeria in the mid-1970s, 12.3
per cent in Morocco, 10.6 per cent in Tunisia, 8.8 per
cent in Yugoslavia, 6.8 per cent in Greece, and 5.2 per
cent in Turkey.[24]

Another way of looking at the same phenomena is
through stocks of non-national residents currently living
in nation states worldwide. Those countries with high
proportions of such members of their societies are ones
that recruited them during the period of industrial expansion after the Second World War, and those that accomplished industrialization through state socialist methods,
involving huge forced movements of population in this
and earlier periods. The oil-rich Arab gulf states are the
clearest example of the former countries: Saudi Arabia,
Kuwait, Oman, Qatar and others had over 50 and up to
90 per cent of non-national residents in 1990, almost all
recruited as workers during their boom years.[25] Conversely, the Central Asian and Baltic republics of the
former USSR had proportions of non-national residents

of between 25 and 50 per cent at that time,[26] as their legacy of Stalinism. The highest rates of non-national residents in Europe were Luxembourg (28 per cent, mostly Portuguese) and Switzerland (18 per cent), both small and extremely prosperous countries, which had brought in unskilled workers during the same period. Proportions in the large EU states – Germany, France, the UK and Italy – were in the range 3 to 8 per cent.[27]

In view of the economic and institutional transformations required by the new model, current flows across borders for settlement and work are therefore modest. The overall numbers living outside their countries of citizenship for over a year represent 2 per cent of the world's population and relate mainly to earlier movements; in other words, 98 per cent remain within state territories.[28] Despite the extraordinary disruptions caused by the collapse of the Soviet Union – the creation of sixteen new 'independent' states, and the imposition of regimes of privatization and market-making on a population of over 200 million – movements of population have come nowhere near those during the comparable disruptions of the immediate postwar years. Given the simultaneous transformations from statist to more open regimes in most developing countries, and the impact of new agricultural and industrial technologies pushed through by transnational corporate interests, the relative stability of populations within borders is the surprising phenomenon.

In relation to refugee flows, the great mass of these stem from specific civil wars and inter-ethnic conflicts. At the peak of world asylum-seeking movements in 1992–3, over 12 million of the nearly 19 million refugees worldwide came from Afghanistan, Israel/Palestine, the former Yugoslavia, Mozambique and the Horn of Africa.[29] Similarly, of the rather higher numbers living within their countries as internally displaced persons, in refugee-like conditions, over 16 million were in Sudan, South Africa, Mozambique, Somalia, the Philippines and Burma.[30] Serious civil conflicts, both acute and longstanding, therefore account for most such movements, and these are principally to neighbouring states, or even contained within those societies' borders.

Another aspect of the current migration 'wave' is the alleged growth of 'illegal immigration'. By definition this is impossible to measure accurately, but again the actual numbers estimated are fairly modest. There were reckoned to be some 4 to 5 million irregular migrants in the USA[31] and about the same number in the European Union[32] in the 1990s. In all, 1.8 million people have availed themselves of amnesties and regularization programmes in the EU since the 1970s;[33] such programmes are a feature of the southern European member states' regimes, since they recognized that they have changed from being countries of emigration to ones of immigration.[34]

The so-called 'world migration crisis' is therefore not about unprecedented movement of populations across borders, but about the principles and rules under which they should move, and how these are agreed and enforced. In the nineteenth century, mass emigration from Europe to the USA and Australasia was consensual among the states concerned, and based on the perception of common interests over the rapid growth of population in a relatively crowded continent, on the one hand, and expanding opportunities and territories in the new worlds, on the other. In the period after the Second World War, both recruitment of workers for First World and oil-rich economies, and the 'nation-building' of newly independent developing ones, could occur within a set of broadly compatible interests. In other words, even though migrant populations themselves often moved because of economic deprivation or political oppression, and often suffered greatly in their processes of transition, states could allow or encourage such 'autonomous' migrations without serious conflicts between them.

The present situation is far more complex than this. The period when First World countries were most restrictive about immigration (so-called 'zero immigration policies' in Europe), starting when economic growth rates fell sharply from their postwar boom levels in the early 1970s, seems now to be coming to an end. For example, both EU member states and the Commission have announced schemes for recruiting high-skilled and unskilled workers from outside the Union.[35] But at the same time, both governments and the Commission have tightened up measures against irregular migration,[36] and adopted still tougher regimes for asylum seekers. Recruitment schemes will allow access for migrants as workers, seen as making positive contributions to the host economy, because they are needed in specific sectors, can be flexibly deployed, and are capable of paying their dues in terms of taxes. Irregulars and asylum seekers are perceived as threats to labour-market regulation and wage protection, to social stability and racial harmony, as evading tax and social contributions, or falling as costs upon state revenues. Migration regimes intentionally discriminate between applicants for entry, even when they have similar social and economic characteristics (see pp. 24–6), to control overall numbers.

These economic arguments for a dual-track approach to immigration policy in First World countries are highly congruent with the model for integration of the world economy espoused by international organizations. But they leave unresolved a great many questions about political membership, and the relation between democratic governance and economic status. They also fail to address moral issues over freedom, equality and justice posed by migrations from regions of the globe that are falling behind the prosperity of the First World, and experiencing internal divergence between the fortunes of winners and losers from globalization.[37] In other words, the crisis arises not from the extent of world migration movements, but from the lack of a political rationale for integrating them; for reconciling them with either humanitarian demands for protection, or ethical principles of distribution; and for the internal rules of membership of liberal democratic states. Furthermore, the diversity and complexity of migration processes in an integrated world economy challenge policy makers to frame consistent rules, and apply them fairly to a whole range of different kinds of migrants.

Migration systems

One of the themes of migration studies in the past twenty-five years has been the disagreement between those who explain flows primarily in terms of 'push and pull' factors, generated by disparities in wages and living standards between states and regions, and those who adopt explanations based on historical political, economic and cultural links between particular sending and receiving countries.[38] There can be little doubt that geographical patterns over time owe more to the latter than the former factors. However, understanding the ways in which the flows of people in particular immigration categories and occupational groups between the countries of a region form a system[39] demands an economic analysis, and it is such systems that are now emerging all over the world.

The most recent of these has developed in East Asia, the fastest-growing region in the world economy up to the time of the financial crisis of 1997. The indigenous rural supplies of labour that fuelled export-orientated industrialization, first in Japan and then in Taiwan and South Korea, and finally in China's Special Economic Zones, could continue to satisfy demand for these workers only in the last of these countries, after each initial phase of rapid expansion. In Hong Kong and Singapore, there was never such an indigenous supply, so from the start they relied on recruitment from abroad. The stock of nonnationals in the region rose from about one million in the early 1980s to over three million in 1996–7.[40] Recruitment of foreign labour, first from South Korea to Japan, then of ethnic Koreans from China to South Korea, from the Philippines and Thailand to Taiwan, and from Indonesia to Malaysia, was initially to smaller firms, providing the flexibility for the industrialization process.[41]

By the mid-1990s, over 100,000 long-term migrants a year were moving into the East Asian countries, and around two-thirds of these were migrating within the region.[42] However, research challenges the notion that this system represents a *regional* integration of the East Asian economies, related to uneven development, unequal wage levels and the sequence of industrialization processes. This would imply that migration systems appear and disappear, as such regional sequences work their way through. Each country changes from being a net labour exporter to a net importer before achieving migration equilibrium, as economic development progresses.[43] Instead, the evidence suggests that migration flows reflect a hierarchy of economies, with dominance determined by each country's position in the structure of the global system, and indicated by inward investment flows, with Japan and the USA as the leading regional investors.[44] It also points to the key role of global cities and city states (Tokyo, Singapore, Hong Kong, Taipei and Seoul) as financial centres and corporate head-quarters, channelling movements of capital and labour, and attracting their own distinctive migration flows.[45]

This is shown by patterns of recruitment to various categories of employment in the system. These are structured by social institutions that link particular states, for specific types of worker. Thus, for instance, although industrial workers are recruited in the linkages listed above, unskilled service and domestic workers flow from the Philippines to the more developed states of the whole region, and from Indonesia to Malaysia and Singapore. In the 'dragon economies', the main recruitment now is of these service workers, along with highly skilled professionals, managers and technical experts, from all the other countries in the top echelon of the global hierarchy.[46] Thus, for example, the leading groups of non-nationals in Hong Kong in 1996 were from the Philippines (almost all domestic service workers) at 128,800, followed by those from the USA, the UK, Canada, Australia, Japan and India. Malaysia, Thailand and Indonesia were the only countries that were represented in the next group with 20,000 to 35,000 each.[47]

All this suggests that migration reinforces a hierarchical structure of economies in both world and regional systems of investment and trade, and reflects the dominance of the leading global actors, through their corporate agents. It also indicates that migration reinforces income inequalities through the recruitment of certain nationalities and ethnicities to domestic and other menial service roles. This follows stereotypes of which such groups are 'suitable' to be servants, sex workers or carers, and leads to a highly structured and differentiated regional division of migrant labour, relating to the demands of global cities and their fast-expanding hinterlands. These policies have been developed under authoritarian regimes, most of which put 'Asian values' above human rights and liberties, and seek to establish Asian national identities with homogeneous civil societies, treating the category of 'immigrant' as socially problematic.[48] In this way, migration serves to consolidate the divergence between the opportunities and lifestyles of a nomadic global elite of finance, industry and high-skilled services, and those of migrants from developing countries who, whatever their educational background or work experience, are seen as natural subordinates and fit for obedient service.

We would argue that similar features are to be found in the migration systems of the North American and Caribbean Basin region, of the Middle East, and between Western and Central-Eastern Europe. New regimes for legal migration enable both top-level and high-skilled nomadism throughout the global economy, and the recruitment of adaptable, biddable, low-paid, seasonal, temporary and service workers. This pattern does not challenge the model of economic integration and global governance set out in the previous chapter; it enables and promotes it. But it does challenge liberal democratic principles of freedom, equality and justice in membership, by selecting according to economic criteria that polarize the incomes and rights of immigrants, and add to the inequalities and injustices within such societies.

It is therefore no coincidence that such features are most clearly evident in the East Asian region, where most newly formed or newly independent states have been unabashed about their nation-building ethnic identities and in their authoritarian methods, and where substantial rights of social citizenship have been minimal. But, as we show in the rest of this chapter and the following one, the global agenda of the new model exerts strong pressures on all governments to move in these directions – those with the weakest economies to send out these forms of labour, and those with the strongest to recruit through these channels.

'Globalization from below' and transnational networks

The processes analysed in the previous section take for granted the mobility of capital established under global financial regimes; the organizational adaptations of companies that allowed the emergence of giant transnational corporations; the policies of governments committed to competing over investment by these firms in export-led industrialization; and the technological innovations that allow businesses with headquarters on one side of the world to carry out production on the other. All these have been factors in the dominance during the last quarter-century of capital over labour, which organizes at a national and local level, and relies on institutions designed and sponsored by states. The emergence of the East Asian economies as industrialized challengers in world markets reflects the decline in the power of organized labour in Europe, North America and Australasia.

However, this dominance of capital also evokes a response, both from small-scale entrepreneurs and from workers, who are able to use the advantages of flexibility that stem from informal structures, and take opportunities created by the new globalized environment. This is reflected both in thriving informal sectors within all kinds of economies worldwide, comprising relatively sophisticated and high-value production as well as low-cost output and ethnic niches,[49] and in the emergence of 'transnational communities', involving dense and multi-stranded networks in transactions in both directions across borders,[50] and allowing the emergence of a kind of grassroots 'globalization from below' that mirrors capitalist development.

This process is enabled by the presence in First World and newly industrializing countries of those workers recruited in the earlier waves of migration, during the 1950s and 1960s in Europe, during the 1970s and 1980s in the USA, and more recently within East Asia. As informal businesses are set up by entrepreneurs in both sending and receiving countries, links between these supply the potential for advantageous cross-border trade and a transnational division of labour, using social capital as a substitute for the financial resources enjoyed by corporations.[51] Researchers give examples of these developments between Central America and the Caribbean islands, on the one hand, and the USA, on the other ('tropical capitalism'), with remittances from the latter used to invest in production in the home country, and agents shuttling between the two for trade and business development.[52] Similar networks have been identified between Taiwan and Hong Kong, on the other hand, and the USA, Europe and Australia, on the other.[53]

Our own researches in London,[54] and those of others in Amsterdam,[55] have analysed Turkish garment factories, which respond with very rapid cross-border adaptations to each change in costs and prices between home and host economies. These rely on a mixture of formal and informal systems, recruiting some migrants under trade union wages and conditions, who pay taxes and social insurance contributions, and others who are undocumented, and are often also drawing social assistance benefits, who are paid at far lower rates. These enterprises recruit from Turkey through trusted agents, rely on communal and family loyalties to sustain trust and suppress conflict, and switch production quickly between sites and countries.[56] In London, they also recruited a mixture of irregular migrants, including large numbers from Poland.[57]

It is particularly difficult for the authorities – those who enforce immigration rules, labour-market regulations, tax and social-insurance regimes and criminal order – to control these activities, because they are so fluid and amorphous, and rely on networks of trust. On the whole, it seems that in most countries they make rather little attempt to do so. In our research in London, owners of 'sweatshops' were given polite warnings about flagrant breaches of all these regulations.[58] This is partly because, although transnational enterprise of this kind is a form of grassroots resistance to top-down globalization, it is also highly complementary to it, using many of the same technologies, communications and transport links, and meeting demands and tastes generated by international capitalism. Far from threatening the dominant economic system, it helps to humanize it by allowing it to adapt better to the circumstances of migratory lives.

'Transnational spaces'

These developments raise the question of whether migrants are creating a whole sphere of social and economic interactions that transcends the political economy of the new model sponsored by international organizations. Do the activities and networks that comprise transnational communities and globalization from below represent a new way of life that is lived not so much within political communities as between them? And if so, can such membership devices as dual citizenship extend the reach of political institutions so as to include this way of life, promote its economic flourishing, and reconcile it with the requirements of the wider system of global governance?

Those who claim great significance for the emergence of these phenomena refer to them as 'transnational social spaces'.[59] The concept arises mainly from the study of groups (such as North Africans in France and Turks and Kurds in Germany) with extended histories of settlement, who have retained and developed their cultural and economic links with their homelands, including (in some cases) their political loyalties and commitments. This research shows that there are forms of social and economic organization that bridge between sedentary populations in the sending and receiving countries, and between their political systems. Hence '. . . migration and re-migration may not be definite, irrevocable and irreversible decisions – transnational lives in themselves may become a strategy for survival and betterment. . . . The transnational social spaces inhabited by immigrants and refugees and immobile residents in both countries thus supplement the international space of sovereign nation states.'[60]

This concept serves primarily as a theoretical device for distinguishing between types of interaction among migrants, for analysing how these are sustained, and for addressing their implications for political membership. For example, kinship groups are sustained by ties of reciprocity and give rise to remittances from migrant workers to family members in home countries; transnational trade and business circuits make use of insider advantages in ethnic groups in host economies to sustain their links across borders; and diasporas maintain cultural solidarity through religious and ideological exchanges.[61] All these have implications for relationships within the receiving countries. 'Transnationalization' defies notions of assimilation and acculturation to the national 'core', and goes beyond the ethnic pluralism of multicultural membership. It suggests that dual or multiple forms of nationality and citizenship might better reflect and recognize the realities of these socio-economic systems.

Furthermore, new organizations for migrants – including irregular migrants and undocumented workers[62] – provide a basis for mobilization and collective struggle that transcends nationality. Although 'transnationalism from below' can be opportunistic and entrepreneurial,[63] it can also be oppositional, reflecting popular resistance that overcomes religious and ethnic differences. It includes networks between campaigns and conferences on issues such as regularizations.

The questions for political membership raised by these phenomena are certainly important, and will be discussed in the final two chapters. But their economic significance should not be exaggerated. Just as migration itself is a response to the 'economic cliffs' (differences in the levels of wages, prices and cultural preferences) that occur at national borders, so transfers, trade, smuggling and a whole division of labour arise to mediate between communities on either side of these boundaries. After a lengthy period of settlement, sedentary members of each community come to enjoy location-specific insider advantages – the extra salaries and non-monetary benefits they gain from inside knowledge, and the social capital generated by their employments and associations in their localities. But each community also shares cultural goods and preferences with the other, creating opportunities for profitable business in production geared to trade between them. Such businesses thrive on migration restrictions, which raise the costs of moving from one country to another for work and settlement. The transnational spaces they create are not transcendent examples of post-national developments, but opportunistic enterprises that make money by brokering blocked or obstructed exchanges, and providing a kind of arbitrage where the mechanics of equilibration are clunky. Open borders would not facilitate these forms of transnationalism; they would eliminate them.

Irregular migration

Similarly, irregular migration is not the expression of a suppressed demand for new forms of transnational membership, but a strategy for dealing with restricted political freedoms, or limited economic opportunities, and controls on border crossings. The globalist model of governance is incoherent about the criteria for regulating these movements. For states whose economies are structurally disadvantaged within the global system, it offers blueprints for managing their dependence with the minimum of damage to the interests of their populations. It allows First World transnational corporations long-term dominance over Second and Third World enterprises, and requires states to organize their labour markets in the ways that best suit these relationships. It gives access to public infrastructures of all states to such corporations, putting their economic interests above any possible political goals that states might prefer to pursue. Citizens of post-communist and developing countries are not unaware of the differences in freedoms and opportunities between their own and First World states, or of differences within their regions. If they are denied access to work and residence in those other countries by immigration rules, some of them will find ways of entering illegally.

The ways in which they do this are very diverse, and are shaped by receiving societies' immigration rules, enforcement practices, labour-market regulation systems and public-service infrastructures. For example, to survive in the highly regulated societies of northern Europe demands skills in networking with settled migrants and nationals to find hosts, sponsors and brokers over accommodation and employment. Our researches in Germany showed that those who arrive as 'tourists' or 'students' needed reliable long-term support of this kind because of elaborate and effective controls over registration for residence, and the regulation of employment and social insurance contributions.[64] Only with such help could they find niches within this society, and eventually strategies (such as marriage) for longer-term settlement.[65] By contrast, in southern European countries, it is rather easy for migrants to enter and survive in the informal economy of street-trading and petty enterprise, but far more difficult to gain access to formal employment and residence permits. Amnesties and regularization programmes have allowed such transitions, but they are implemented through highly discretionary and clientelist practices in the relevant agencies.[66] Finally, in the UK (and to an extent also the USA), much more open and less regulated labour markets and accommodation systems allow ready access for migrants, once they get through restrictive entry processes; but survival in the shadow world of irregulars is a hazardous business. Our researches in London revealed relations of unrestrained competition between migrants, including reporting each other to the immigration authorities because of rivalry for jobs, or as part of quarrels.[67]

As a result of this, the adaptations required by irregular status in these countries are quite different, and migrants from the same society can both self-select and be moulded into quite varied patterns. Brazilians in Berlin were far more likely to become entertainment and sex workers, domestic cleaners and marriage partners than were Brazilians in London, who could easily get work in hotels, bars, restaurants, cafés and fast-food outlets.[68] Conversely, Bra-

zilians in London were more likely to be registered as
students, but not to attend classes; their 'schools' were
merely brokering this immigration status, which allowed
them to be undocumented workers.[69] Poles in Italy and
Greece were more likely to be middle-aged women, who
worked as live-in carers for rich, elderly nationals,[70] and
in the UK to be young, well educated, ambitious and
market-orientated, to work in minority-ethnic-owned factories, in catering or construction.[71]

Irregular migration challenges both the new model for
global governance and the older model of national welfare
states. Its challenge to the new model lies in exposing the
lack of a rationale or mechanism for balancing the requirements of 'flexibility' in labour markets with the need for
'activation' to mobilize the workforces within states. Flexibility implies that employers can hire whoever is able to
do the work at the lowest cost, on terms that allow them
to be deployed most profitably, including short-term, part-
time, occasional or seasonal work; and that they can hire
them directly or through agencies, and give them contracts
as employees or pay them as self-employed agents. But
activation implies that the state should take measures to
make their working-age populations as skilled and educated as possible, well prepared and motivated for whatever employment is available, and adaptable to changing
demand for their work.

If employers can achieve the greatest flexibility and
lowest costs by hiring workers from abroad, but states
must optimize the education and training of workforces
for the domestic labour market, then there is a potential
conflict of interests between them. States will adopt immigration restrictions to promote the maximum employment
of their populations, and employers will defy these restrictions to hire migrants where this is to their advantage,
unless the risks of detection and the costs of defection are

high. The employment of irregular migrants, especially by marginal entrepreneurs, is one clear reflection of this tension. Another is high rates of unemployment in the domestic workforce among nationals who (because of family commitments or accommodation costs, for example) cannot compete with migrant labour for the wages being offered by employers. A third is expensive state training schemes for unemployed nationals, co-existing with shadow labour markets for both nationals and irregular immigrants.

The new model of global governance does not indicate how First World states might resolve these issues by balancing recruitment (especially of unskilled workers) with activation of their less adaptable and mobile populations. Nor does it tell post-communist or developing countries how to ensure that their best-educated and -trained workers do not quit the country (causing a brain drain[72]), leaving less productive and innovative nationals as their home workforces. Irregular migration does seem to select more able as well as more adventurous agents,[73] with the wasteful outcome of high-skilled people doing menial tasks for low pay in shadow markets. New policies for recruiting 'flexible, adaptable, temporary workers'[74] provide some easing of the tensions between these principles, but do not provide coherent solutions to the basic issues.

In their own terms, welfare states offered more coherent answers to these questions. Labour markets were not simply competitive; they required institutions to restrain competition as well as to promote it, for the sake of protecting overall living standards, and promoting the growth of productivity. The state was in a better position to supply unemployment insurance than either private firms or private insurance companies, or workers themselves, because it had more resources and a better overview of the labour market. But state unemployment insurance might make it too easy for employers to lay off workers. This made a case for employment protection; employers were required to make severance payments as a kind of compensation to the state for the protection it offered their workers against unemployment. Finally, minimum wages acted as a barrier against exploitation, especially by firms that dominate local labour markets. In a one-company town with high costs for moving, workers might be paid far less than their productivity demanded; the combination of employment protection and minimum wages therefore raised the reservation wage of low-skilled workers, and put a premium on measures to improve their productivity, rather than either exploiting them or sacking them.[75]

However, such analyses make sense only in a context of labour markets conceived as national institutions, organized for the benefit of citizens. From a global perspective, these are exactly the kinds of institutional arrangements that give rise to 'economic cliffs' between states, and to pressures for irregular migration into the most successful systems for national protection. Once such institutions are in place, they have a logic of their own, and create interests in their perpetuation. Germany is the clearest example of this process: when faced with the challenges of slower growth and the absorption of the former GDR, it used social insurance as a way of protecting citizens from the shocks of change, and allowed firms to adapt without the necessary pressures for innovation and creative destruction. The results are far lower flows in and out of jobs, high long-term unemployment, low mobility and very costly retraining schemes that recycle the same people through repeated reprocessing. Only very tight regulation and elaborate enforcement prevent a larger growth of shadow labour markets for irregular migrants, and both agriculture and construction are sustained only by schemes that allow fairly large-scale recruitment of foreign workers.

Irregular migration has therefore provided an important spur to a review of the tensions between labour market institutions, social rights and economic goals, and between the new model of global governance and nation state systems. Along with asylum seeking (often perceived as disguised economic migration[76]), it has brought about the shift in policy that occurred at the start of the new century, and the explicit revision of the relationship between economic and political membership structures.

New forms of economic membership

Modernity began with the creation of new forms of global nomadism. Up to then, only warlords and armed merchant venturers travelled freely across the world (as conquerors, crusaders, explorers and traders). In the modern era new classes of diplomats, politicians, capitalists, artists and scientists moved between states with an ease previously reserved for monarchs and generals. In the present age, the list is being extended, as the new model of global governance demands that more categories of workers move, and stay for longer, than under the rules for transnational corporations and international agencies in the last quarter of the twentieth century. As states open up public infrastructures for global competition, and more internal systems are transformed by international ones, new kinds of global nomadic agents come into being, and need new institutional systems to accommodate them.

These new nomads are not necessarily the highest-paid or most prestigious staff in their organizations. Some of them are very young, and took to this lifestyle immediately after graduating. Some undertake it with the conscious goal of settling later in their countries of origin, after a decade or two of travelling. Some move every few months; others settle for longer, partly because of the demands of their work, in teaching, health care, social work or some other human service occupation.

We conducted research interviews with work permit holders from India and Poland, recruited for employment in the UK in 2001–2.[77] One group of these were staff of financial and business service firms, experts in information technology systems; another were academic scientists; and a third were nurses, employed in private nursing homes and care institutions. The accounts they gave of their reasons for becoming nomadic, their choice of their particular jobs, and their adaptations within UK society gave insight into the new forms of economic membership now available to these groups of agents.

In reviewing their employment options, global nomads compared the advantages and drawbacks of the USA, Europe and East Asia in terms of access to work and residence permits, as well as salaries and living conditions. A software developer from Poland, working on a three-month contract in the UK (arranged by his agent in Vienna), made it clear that the parameters of his working life were set by his employers, irrespective of which country he was in.

> The jobs in Belgium, Amsterdam, Istanbul were contract work for a certain amount of time. . . . I would say those companies don't differ too much. Wherever you go their organization structure and the way of your work is quite similar, . . . it's a bit different, but it's not so much because of the country, it's more because of the type of company.

Another young Polish man, working for a financial company in the City of London, said that he wanted to come to the UK for 'the opportunity to . . . get to know how it is working in . . . the real capitalistic country where you have to work very hard and where you are judged by the results. . . . [i]f you survive here, then I . . . just think that I would survive everywhere.' Another described how, as a graduate of a business school in Gdansk, he usually met his peer group in the transit lounge at Copenhagen airport, since that was the route through which they all flew to their work destinations, and some of them would be certain to meet there on any day that they were undertaking a journey home or to a new contract.

Indian technical experts and academic scientists retained strong links with families back home, and also received visits from family members. But – like Polish nomads – they chose to live in middle-class white English neighbourhoods, rather than those with settled UK Indian populations. As an Indian IT worker explained, 'It's an English, a small English residential area. I live within that. And I think it's a better idea to live [there] than to live in a community, where you tend to become more, er, you tend to – what do you say? – become more inward. . . .'

Both Indian and Polish work permit holders belonged to white middle-class English cultural and leisure clubs, or joined their firms' sports clubs. Their good pay and their employment in these well-endowed companies gave them access to collective facilities they and their families needed for their quality of life. It was their links to physical capital, through their jobs, not their social capital as members of immigrant communities, that supplied their cultural infrastructures. They enjoyed good relationships with white English colleagues and neighbours, being able to buy straight into work-based facilities and residential communities of choice. This contrasted with both Turkish and Kurdish asylum seekers, who relied on social capital in political and cultural associations from their home countries, and irregular migrants from Poland and Brazil, with their confinement to small groups of trusted friends, and fears of betrayal by treacherous fellow migrants.

Indian nurses were in a slightly different position, because of limited pay, and more demanding work conditions. They were called on to do practical tasks of care not required of professional staff in their home countries. They also could afford to live only in more modest accommodation, often in hostels attached to their workplaces. What was striking about their accounts was the way they described the global scope of professional job opportunities, and how it was for the chance of such nomadism that they had entered their training. One, whose family were almost all nomads in one profession or another, said: 'I took nursing because my aunt was a nurse, . . . she works in America, so I wanted to go to America, so that's why I did it, nursing.' This sounds more like the motive for becoming a merchant seaman in an earlier era.

The human service professions are now the largest category of recruitment of foreign staff under the UK work permit scheme.[78] Several factors contribute to supply problems in these occupations. In nursing, for example, as in teaching, there are enough trained UK nationals to fill all posts, but the pay is not sufficient to retain them;[79] many earn more by entering other occupations (or working abroad). Those with family commitments often cannot afford to live in the cities where their services are required, or refuse to live in deprived districts where they could afford such family accommodation. There is competition between public services and commercial employers, some of whom are expanding with the long-term aim of competing for overseas contracts. Foreign recruits often come on temporary appointments, and are able to live cheaply in shared accommodation; their salaries, though modest, are well above those they would earn in their home countries. In all these respects, these arrangements prefigure the situation worldwide, as public services are opened up for competition between corporations, creating a far larger class of these global nomads.

Conclusions

New forms of global economic nomadism have outstripped the capacities of national migration management systems to adapt to the requirements of international capitalism. The young Polish software developer quoted above spent most of his interview complaining about the absurdities of the immigration rules and procedures of most European countries, especially Germany. He found it ridiculous that companies there were required to advertise vacancies locally, when everyone in the industry knew that the labour market for these skills was a global one. In order to cope with the delays caused by such anachronistic practices, he and his colleagues were forced to break the rules by various ruses and stratagems, such as

> working as freelance consultants. So the companies are registered somewhere else, either in the US, because their taxation is low there, some of them register their company in Poland and they just direct themselves to do the job. It's actually not, not legal to do it, but any companies which are hiring them know that there's no other way . . . this is one of the examples where the US is ahead of Europe.

Global nomadism explicitly rejects the notion that labour markets are national institutions, constructing relationships between citizens for the sake of equity as well as efficiency, and designed to absorb economic shocks as self-contained systems. It substitutes a version in which open labour markets allow agents with skills from all over the world to compete on equal terms, without regard to nationality. In such institutions, people change jobs and locations very frequently, and require an infrastructure that allows the costs of such transitions to be minimized. Firms that provide short-lease apartments, leisure facilities, gymnasia and sports clubs meet many such needs; accessible residential districts with good schools and health clinics provide for travelling family members. In this way, the economic systems that demand global nomadism also supply the facilities for its collective needs of membership. Nation states are under pressure to streamline their work permit processes to keep up with these changes, which bear little relation to political membership categories.

From the other end of globalization processes, irregular migration exerts its own pressures. Migrants who do low-paid service work in shadow labour markets want to be able to return home from time to time without risking detection. They are motivated to regularize more for the chance to broaden their economic opportunities than to join a political community. Irregular Polish migrants in the UK can achieve these aims through the business visa scheme.[80] Drawing on their contacts in the shadow economy, they supply accountants and solicitors with the materials for a 'business plan' that then entitles them to a visa, so long as they can get a National Insurance number to legitimate their proposed enterprise, and to show that they intend to pay taxes and insurance contributions. Asked about these prospectuses, two commented:

> It's all fiction. I have never seen the business plan myself. I don't even know what's written there.

He [accountant] listens to what you want to include and then adds his own ideas, so in the end it's more his business plan than yours.

Another explained that his visa described him as a provider of culturally sensitive funeral services for Polish war veterans. This did not require any capital, as he could use English funeral directors, and simply supply a Polish flag and translation facilities. He had not actually arranged any funerals; he earned his living as a minicab driver.[81]

Irregular migrants who can regularize by such routes, or through marriage, or some other process, thus become transnational economic agents, with access to social as well as labour-market resources. But although they do not share the collective facilities enjoyed by global nomads through their links to corporate agencies, they can enter society as mainstream members, linked through public services with national populations, without the need to join the political community. Here again, economic systems provide the key to migrant strategies of access, and a flexible supply of adaptable workers or employers within national labour markets.

In all these respects, migration patterns at the start of the twenty-first century are more congruent with the new model of global governance than they are in conflict with it. There are tensions, but the model displaces these onto national governments. The model has no mechanism for balancing the supply of workers with appropriate skills from national populations and recruitment of similarly qualified or less skilled workers from abroad. It demands that all states make their populations as employable as possible, but leaves it to open labour markets to resolve who should be employed where, and to governments to make the rules about movements between them. It has nothing to say about political membership – either the problems of those fleeing from political persecution, or the issues of how migrants gain access to the rights of citizenship. This leaves states with thorny questions about how to determine claims for humanitarian protection, and how to provide for those nationals unable to secure the means of subsistence within their home labour markets.

The emergence of migration management regimes reflects these unresolved dilemmas. Movements across borders are part of a global upsurge in mobility of people, both within and between states, whose ultimate significance is still hard to assess. Migration management regimes steer and facilitate some of the new forms of global nomadism, and try to block others. Nomads are both innovators and throwbacks to earlier epochs; they challenge boundaries and pioneer new social relations.[82]

In the next chapter we turn to the issues of coherence between economic and political membership raised in this one. Can liberal democratic principles allocate access to First World societies in ways that are consistent with internal standards of equality and justice? And can the kinds of economic membership required by the new model of global governance be reconciled with any version of democratic citizenship?

4

Cosmopolitan Economic Membership

In this chapter, we turn to the ethical evaluation of regimes for national protection, global governance and federal restructuring. We argue that the dominant ethical perspective on social relationships, liberalism, is incoherent on questions of organizational boundaries, and the dominant justification of collective authority, democracy, cannot say how members should be selected. This leaves liberal democrats (and egalitarians generally) with no basis for evaluating migration regimes, the regulation of mobility or the organization of membership.

The central principle of liberal democracy is the moral equality of persons.[1] The duty to treat each as of equal concern is the basis for theories of justice.[2] 'In a liberal polity all are at the same time equally subjects and sovereigns; they are equally subject to the law and at the same time those laws must be the expression of their sovereign will as citizens.'[3] But the other fundamental principle is that all have equal freedom to choose their own version of the good life, in ways that do not infringe the same freedom for others. In Rawls's theory of justice, 'freedom of movement and free choice of occupation against a background of diverse opportunities' are part of the 'basic structure of society'.[4] Such fundamental liberties have priority over all other principles. They cannot be constrained in order to influence economic outcomes, or to protect some cultural goods of the community.

Equal citizenship and free movement can be reconciled in this theory of justice only by its silence on the question of boundaries. The goods of such a political community end at its borders, which are taken as given. There is no theoretical justification of exclusion, because outsiders are invisible.[5] Since there is nothing to say about non-members, there can be no liberal democratic criteria for admission to membership. But that leaves the theory incoherent between internal and external relations.[6] How can any rule select between applicants for entry who are morally identical with each other, and with members? How can any rule be legitimately imposed on applicants, who have played no democratic part in making it?[7]

Either principles of equality and justice are not universal, but apply only to members of bounded communities, and not beyond borders; or they are universal, and demand open borders. Those who try to find universal principles for selective admission to citizenship point to features of nations that give members special ethical claims on each other.[8] But ethical communities straddle borders, and nations are not ethical communities; exclusions based on national identity or culture are either inconsistent versions of communitarianism,[9] or illiberal protections for monoculturalism.[10] Alternatively, those who acknowledge that selection is inconsistent with universal liberal values, because it is necessary to protect liberal democracy as a vulnerable political system,[11] concede that its principles cannot extend to the international order, and can provide no moral rules for relations between states, or between states and applicants for membership.[12]

However, this incoherence between liberal democracy's internal and external principles can be resolved rather easily. The first step is to recognize that moral equality among members is appropriate to the political domain and the practice of citizenship. The second is to accept that free movement and choice over where to live and work are accommodated within markets, and appropriate for the economic sphere. This allows a dual or twin-track approach – political communities, with distinctive national versions of equality and justice among members, and cosmopolitan economic membership, in an integrated world market system.

The key to this resolution lies in property rights. Libertarians have long recognized that, if the entire globe were made up of private property, contractual relationships and market transactions, there would be no contradictions between principles of individual moral sovereignty and decisions about admissions to membership.[13] Populations would simply sort themselves into communities of choice, achieving exclusions through the price mechanism, and governing themselves consensually through contractual agreements. The problem thus lies in defining the role of the overall political authority and its public infrastructure, so that political membership can be reconciled with these personal liberties and property entitlements.

Yet in practice, freedom of economic movement and exclusion from membership co-exist in all societies, both internally and externally. Individuals with identical sets of formal civil rights belong to quite different business organizations, residential neighbourhoods, occupational pensions schemes, health insurance plans, private clubs and cultural facilities.[14] Exclusion from such memberships operates through their admission fees, contribution requirements, annual dues or accommodation prices. Selection is accomplished through the cost of entry, and individuals are excluded if they cannot afford to pay. Such exclusions from economic membership are impeccably liberal, so it is only a matter of reconciling these processes with territorial and administrative governance to achieve the necessary coherence.

This approach, which has underpinned the programme for globalization, and the new model of governance sponsored by the IMF, the World Bank, the WTO and other international organizations, subordinates one part of the liberal democratic tradition to another. It gives priority to rights to freedom of choice over rights to equality of voice; and it gives priority to the property rights of those with assets and skills over the moral claims of those with vulnerabilities and needs. It justifies itself by appealing to its potential for enhancing global economic growth, and hence global welfare. But it produces growing inequality of incomes and of freedoms. Ultimately, it undermines the foundations for all progressive political movements since the eighteenth century, and provides new justifications for serfdom.

All this is achieved in the name of liberal democracy, by releasing the hidden power of markets and property rights. Price provides the criterion for differentiating between 'desirable' and 'undesirable' members, both of internal associations, and in relation to external applicants. Ability to pay and potential to contribute select suitable from unsuitable candidates. Such selections do not discriminate on grounds of skin colour, gender or any other arbitrary feature. They allow free movement and choice of the good way of life under conditions of liberal neutrality.

This leaves to the political realm a number of residual but important questions of power in relationships between mobile and sedentary agents. Which infrastructural goods can economic membership groups and communities of choice not be relied upon to supply for themselves contractually to the optimum level? Which externalities arise in relationships between such organizations and communities that require regulation? And – above all – which individuals cannot afford the entry price for *any* such associations and communities of choice, and what should be done with them?

It is this last question that is shaping both the social policies of nation states and their responses to asylum seeking. Cosmopolitan economic membership is an 'invisible hand' process that allows selection and exclusion to take place without overt regulation. Like movements in markets, such flows and clusters appear to occur spontaneously and naturally, and produce outcomes that are 'unpatterned'[15] and voluntary. They seem to allow 'order without control'.[16] But they rely on rules that are in reality harsh and coercive.

In a system of membership based on property-holdings, prices and contribution fees, those without the ability to pay the admission charges become costs on those who can. Not only are there vast inequalities between the facilities of the various organizations and communities; there is an even larger fundamental difference of status between those who are included in some form of economic membership and those who are not. For the latter, their human vulnerabilities and needs become redefined as disqualifications. Instead of having moral claims on the political community, as members or as 'necessitous strangers', their needs condemn them to be reclassified as morally defective.

Moral claims and human needs

Moral equality and distributive justice in liberal democratic theory are linked by fragile bonds of membership. The political community is a system of legitimation and distribution among members with recognizable moral claims. In Rawls's theory of justice, the Liberty Principle includes all those with capacities for rationality and moral action, the Equal Opportunity Principle opens offices and positions to all under conditions of fair equality, and the Difference Principle rules that inequalities must benefit the least advantaged.[17] The material claims of the least advantaged therefore rest on their access to the status of fully rational moral members.

In a world with nation states as the legitimate distributive units of membership, claims from human needs, leading to income transfers and social services, were based on the claimants' relative position as citizens. The 'least advantaged' from the perspective of national welfare states were their citizens in greatest need, with fewest resources. But cosmopolitan economic membership refers to the whole world as an integrated economy, and a system for maximum growth in global welfare through free trade and free movement. In such a system, there is a built-in assumption that the rules of mobility in markets benefit the least advantaged. In any case, the relevant needy populations (the 'worst off' who should benefit from material inequalities) are surely those scratching a subsistence in Africa, Asia or remote parts of Latin America, and who make no direct claims from their needs. Those who do make such claims, either nationals who fail to support themselves and their dependants and hence reveal and rely upon their lack of skills and adaptability to the requirements of their local economies, or foreigners who move across borders without having the skills that are demanded in the country they enter, do not have recognizably legitimate moral claims. Theirs are not 'human needs', with ethical force, because they are claims from individual incompetences, or irrational choices.

Liberal theory has a long and dishonourable tradition

of distinctions between those included in the ambit of rationality as free and equal participants, and those who forfeit rights or lie beyond the boundaries of such moral and political relationships because of their behaviour or characteristics.[18] The seventeenth- and eighteenth-century foundational texts of liberalism used such arguments to justify slavery,[19] the subjugation of women to patriarchal power,[20] and the brutalities of physical and capital punishment in criminal corrections.[21] In the nineteenth century, the same arguments included Europeans alone as rational and moral beings;[22] they legitimated imperialism, a limited franchise and the workhouse regime for paupers.[23] Some of these boundaries were drawn on racial lines, others on behavioural ones, and others still on property or poverty.

Modern cosmopolitan liberals drop racial and gender-based reasoning, but still find arguments for why certain individuals forfeit their moral equality through their actions. The paradigm for such arguments is criminal justice: those who violate the property or personal rights of others risk forfeiting their civil and political rights, and their liberty itself. But, by analogy, the same loss of rights was linked in the nineteenth century and beyond to claiming public assistance. A pauper ceased to be a citizen, and could be required to enter the workhouse (losing rights of mobility and free association) and to undertake forced labour. Simply by falling as a cost upon the income and property of fellow members of the political community, poor people surrendered their moral autonomy as well as their democratic sovereignty.[24]

Cosmopolitan economic membership links free movement and entry qualifications for all forms of association to making the required contribution. The material basis for membership is also the moral legitimation for sharing its benefits. Any other form of claim violates neutrality and equality of opportunity by introducing irrelevant grounds for special treatment – national, racial, gender, physical or other characteristics. Hence the boundaries of membership become economic, and human needs become costs, not claims. From that perspective, people who cannot gain access to membership through contributions are a form of negative externality in a global system for maximum production and optimum distribution through markets. Whether they are migrants who claim support as asylum seekers, beggars who intrude upon people's daily business in public places, or nationals incapable of supporting themselves within these systems, they represent either quasi-criminal predations on others' moral entitlements, or 'human trash' who drive down property prices, and force others into unchosen interactions and proximities.[25] Hence this thinking justifies the incarceration of asylum seekers, and the forced labour of able-bodied claimants under schemes for workfare or welfare-to-work activation.

The role of political authority therefore becomes primarily one of enabling the contributions required for economic membership. The systems for education, training and health care it supplies are justified by this goal, which allows all agents to be autonomous actors within the global economy. Those who have had the benefit of such systems have demonstrated a form of moral failure, akin to a crime, in seeking to impose additional costs on others by claiming public assistance. Hence systems of income support (like those for asylum seekers) are justified in coercing them to accept regimes aimed at restoring them to economic independence. These include compulsory education and training in such moral duties as marriage and parenting; they involve removing their benefits or sending them to prison for failing to get their children to school;[26] and, in the case of asylum seekers, keeping them right outside the host society by intercepting their means of transport, or by instant deportation.[27]

In these ways, states' authority in enforcing the 'obligations of citizenship',[28] and excluding those from abroad unable to demonstrate that they are immediately ready and required to shoulder them, are directly in line with the demands of the new international order. Political communities mobilize their members for economic activity, and do not act as obstacles to global transformative processes.

Systems of economic membership

In this chapter, we analyse forms of economic membership, and how they fit with political processes under the new order of global governance. In the spontaneous groupings that occur through markets, agents are seen to be expressing choices about collective goods, as well as organizing themselves for optimal productive contributions. But 'economic membership' is a capacious term that embraces the diverse ways in which groups agree to share costs of collective provision, either by supplying each other with services through reciprocity and co-operation, or by paying others to supply them as employees or contracted providers.

What might count as an economic membership system varies greatly between societies according to their levels of development and extent of state ownership of resources. In the developing world, subsistence and communal systems are the most important such organizatons, and they have again become significant in the post-communist countries. Such activities are local in their reach; they could be seen as 'cosmopolitan' only in the sense that they might be funded or managed by an international NGO, or accountable (through national government) to the IMF or the World Bank.

The new model for global governance seeks to create links between even the most remote and self-contained of such systems and the regulatory order of international finance. Each country that requires assistance from the IMF or the World Bank must submit a Poverty Reduction Strategy Paper (PRSP) to the two agencies' joint International Development Association (IDA) in order to qualify. These allocations will then be 'performance-based', and related to their success in meeting IDA criteria and achieving IDA outcomes. The application for aid will constitute the country's 'business plan', and becomes 'the primary vehicle for comprehensive diagnosis, and for participation and consultation'.[29] This whole process is expected

> to play an increasing role in supporting prioritized policy actions in implementing the country's agenda of social and structural policy and institutional reform. Progress in this regard will be gradual, however, with careful analysis of the appropriateness of the instrument for each individual country particularly in terms of the integrity and transparency of public expenditure management and procurement systems. This approach will allow learning from, and application of, the lessons of experience.[30]

Clearly this approach is tailored to integrate into the global order every level of economic activity in those countries that apply for aid, an order that the international bodies regulate by making governments accountable to them for their institutional design and its performance. The goals for poverty reduction are worthy ones, and the principles rest on sincere beliefs that market-based regulation is the only reliable route to long-term growth. The objectives are the eventual transformation of all states into suitable intermediaries in a world economy that is integrated through these principles, and restructuring all state organizations and activities to these requirements.

In reality, there are still enormous variations in the extent to which countries reflect this model, in their integration in these processes, and in the speed with which they are moving in these directions. For example, in 1998 the Heritage Foundation/*Wall Street Journal*'s *Index of Economic Freedom* (roughly speaking, openness to global markets, and absence of state ownership and intervention) graded countries on a scale of 0 (100 per cent free) to 5 (no freedom). Two states, Cuba and North Korea, still scored 5, and Vietnam 4.70; the Russian Federation 3.45 and China 3.75; France and Italy both 2.50; the UK 1.95 and the USA 1.90; Singapore 1.30 and Hong Kong 1.25.[31] Even similarities of scores on these measures conceal differences between sectors over privatization and the penetration of markets.

However, the objective of the IDA is not confined to reducing the role of the state, or even to transforming its institutional structures and policies. It is also concerned with reducing warlordism and mafia rackets, which force populations into conflicting armies of predation, or traffick them abroad under conditions of bonded labour, or use them to smuggle drugs into other countries. In this sense, it and other international organizations aim to create conditions for free mobility within labour markets globally, including systems for recruitment across borders, to replace the coercion of people for violence and criminal activity, which often spills over into the international system. Cosmopolitan economic membership as an institutional order is presented as the approach that allows peaceful co-ordination of the choices of individual agents, in very diverse productive and distributive systems, through the transformation of states' regimes of governance.

In what follows in this chapter, the analysis is based on the most 'advanced' form of economic development, and the one that most closely approximates to the model prescribed by those agencies. It is the version found in the USA and UK especially, where a post-industrial structure of employment has seen most workers move into service jobs, some of which are highly paid (as in professional work, and in the business and financial services), but many involve low-productivity, labour-intensive tasks of social reproduction (such as routine care of frail elderly people), and therefore do not pay enough to meet the high costs of living and raising a family in such a society. Here the key issue becomes how the political regulation of such a society can sustain the economic membership systems required by the wider order of the global economy, and supply them with the access to resources demanded by corporate agents, and the workers with the skills and motives that are needed for their purposes.

States, cities and membership

The first step in the analysis of how political communities are coming to accommodate cosmopolitan economic membership is to recognize the complexity of systems through which agents move across borders, under rules designed to facilitate transnational economic activities. There are rules for access by companies to ownership of the land, offices and production facilities, to contracts and to markets; for workers to employment; for these and others to residence, and to the associations and clubs that make up civil society; and to systems of personal security and protection against existential risks (both commercial and collective). Many non-nationals who cross borders under one or other of these rules do not need or get the other kinds of access, and the vast majority do not seek political membership of the encompassing state.

These features of cross-border movements are most obvious in 'global cities' – large, cosmopolitan conurbations that serve as headquarters for transnational corporations, as well as regional administrative and financial centres.[32] Such cities are spatially concentrated civil societies, with dense networks of interaction and communication[33] between nationals and non-nationals, neither of whom 'belong' to the city's native-born community of fate, most of whom are likely to be present as a consequence of other decisions (by their companies, over investment or employment, or some other opportunity), and all of whom must adapt to each other as mobile and autonomous agents. Although all rely on a shared infrastructure for these interactions, few are likely to see political membership, either of the city or of the state, as a key resource in their dealings with each other. (This was poignantly underlined in the huge list of nationalities of those killed in the collapse of the World Trade Center on 11 September 2001.)

For both nationals (from all over the state) and non-nationals (from all over the world), selection for admission to these networks is achieved through open markets, in terms of employment opportunities and accommodation prices. This applies also to those who enter the country illegally (by clandestine means or by deception – for instance as tourists or students) and then stay to do undocumented or shadow work in the city's informal economy. Research shows that global cities are a magnet for such workers because of the high demand for unskilled service employers who are adaptable and willing to improvise over accommodation arrangements.[34]

Global cities illustrate the flexibility of cosmopolitan economic membership as the basis for intensive interactions between populations that are interdependent on some dimensions, but entirely disconnected on others. This is because no single principle replaces political membership as the underpinning for their economic exchanges and social relationships. Access for business and employment allows non-nationals to interact with nationals to mutual advantage; access to residence (often temporary) allows for entry to communities of choice and cohabitation with selected neighbours; access to associations and clubs gives membership of civil society; and insurance markets, occupational schemes and public services allow for personal security and protection. City societies can accommodate even quite personal relationships between the wealthy nationals and non-nationals and the irregular entrants whom they employ, for example as live-in nannies, carers and cleaners, through a mixture of private household and market transactions.

From one perspective, therefore, political membership becomes a residual category under cosmopolitan economic systems, and the role of political authority is reduced to simply holding the ring for such interactions. Rights of access allow relationships between highly mobile populations, with transferable assets and skills, and sedentary ones, with fixed assets in land and buildings, living in stable, local communities. The wealth and expertise of some nationals and non-nationals give them advantages over poor and less skilled populations that are somewhat similar to those of colonialists over subject populations in the age of imperialism. What stops them simply buying up a whole quarter (or third, or half) of a city, and rebuilding the infrastructure to suit their global economic purposes, by establishing their own jurisdiction over it? Why should they not then bring in an equally cosmopolitan workforce, setting their own terms for its employment and settlement?

It is clear that world economic integration releases

strong forces that move in these directions. What restrains them is the set of political institutions that transform land and what stands on it into *territory*, people with skills into *labour markets*, associations and groups into *societies*, and resident populations into *citizens*. Free movement within societies was a necessary condition for institutions of equality, justice and democratic governance to be established.[35] But these institutions are also challenged by differentials in wealth and mobility, both within and outside societies. The moral claims of equality under liberal democracy demand a balance between mobility as a means of permeating enclaves (districts, occupations, organizations) based on power and privilege (of class, gender or ethnicity), and mobility as a means of creating alternative enclaves, of wealth, security and exploitation. If the rich are able to find space and social structures from which they can exclude the poor, and if they can set the terms of their relationships with them, then geographical mobility can block social mobility, and local self-rule can prevent equal citizenship.

In the rest of this chapter we will first examine the paradox of autonomy and constraint in the public sphere of liberal democracy. Then we will consider in more detail how the model of governance set out in chapter 2 first enables physical and social segregation between mobile rich and sedentary poor populations to be accomplished, and how this in turn helps legitimate inequalities of status and power, as well as of material resources.

Public sphere and public services in liberal democracy

It has become something of a cliché that the transnational mobility of capital is a constraint on redistribution in social democratic welfare states.[36] The threat to move businesses abroad limits the scope of governments to tax corporate profits, and the potential to shift savings into foreign funds constrains personal taxation. But our analysis goes much further than this, to argue that liberal democratic versions of equality and justice are undermined when populations are able to sort themselves into residential districts and collective systems where members have similar incomes and tastes. This is because the egalitarian element in liberal democracy relies on common interests between a diversity of individuals and groups created by interactions in a shared social environment. Where economic membership accomplishes physical segregation into homogeneous groups, the institutional basis for equality of status is eroded, and the moral arguments for liberal rights are weakened.

The moral equality of human beings in modern liberal democratic theory is not derived from natural rights, or from assumptions about the essential nature of the human species.[37] It is a political construction, based on interactions between morally sovereign individuals in a public space. The political public sphere, where members deliberate and make collectively binding decisions,[38] the economic public sphere, where they are free to pursue private interests within these rules, and the social public sphere, where they enter into a multitude of cross-cutting associations, are all fragile, artificial and largely abstract creations; but they provide the shared context for the common interests that each individual has in the institutions for co-operative human flourishing.

Rights are resources provided by social institutions, allowing those who share interactions within those spheres to participate as members rather than unprotected, unrecognized and unequal individuals.[39] Liberal political rights allow such members the status of equality, despite differences of abilities, assets, tastes, beliefs and interests. Substantial rights confer 'those capabilities that are required for autonomous agency in the public spheres of civil society and for equal membership in the polity'.[40]

This refers to Sen's notion of 'goal rights' as those freedoms that allow individuals to choose the lives they value,[41] and take part in the activities of their communities as full members, recognized as such by those on whom they depend to fulfil them. Such rights translate human 'functionings' (such as being in good physical and psychological health) into 'capabilities' to achieve the goals that they have chosen, and thus wellbeing.[42] Since individuals always rely on interactions with others for the achievement of their goals, these rights allow them to enter into such relationships without unjust handicaps to such recognition. Without a public sphere that allows members to exercise their capabilities for free and responsible actions in relation to each other, these can neither be learned nor demonstrated, and the whole justification of liberal democratic membership – its basis in moral equality and autonomy – becomes vulnerable.

Institutions are therefore required to link the substantial elements of rights that redistribute resources for the sake of equalizing capabilities of members, and rights of equal access to the collective infrastructure of society, to the actual processes of interaction between members of that society. Institutions must provide opportunities for members of society to experience others as equal participants, to treat each other with respect and concern, to communicate about the issues that arise in such interactions, and to resolve conflicts of interests satisfactorily. In liberal democracy, the practice of equal membership is not a primary duty or an overriding priority, as in the civic republican tradition;[43] individuals are quite entitled to abstain from political activity, and to withdraw into private life.[44] Because of the intentional diversity of conceptions of the good life and how to lead it, and the multiplicity of cultural associations in civil society, there are few rituals or rallies through which liberal democrats can live out together their commitment to principles of equality and justice.

This is why public services come to have such enormous significance under liberal democracy, despite liberalism's ambivalence about the 'coercive' elements in taxation, redistribution and collective provision. Without schools in which children for all sections of society can learn to be members together, how can the qualities for these particular interactions be acquired? Without work in the public services – for health, for social care, and for emergencies like fires and accidents – how can concern for the common good of all members be expressed? And without the opportunities to meet and communicate that are afforded by schools, hospitals, clinics, libraries, parks, post offices, polling booths and public transport systems, how can members of society interact together in the very particular way that gives the values of liberal democracy substance?

Hence the paradox of liberal democracy, that the kind of individual autonomy it constructs can only be achieved within a certain set of institutional constraints that shape actions and create interdependence. Society cannot work in accordance with principles of equality and justice unless members can both contribute to the common good through working in public services, and experience their common interests in moral equality through using public services. Freedom must therefore be actualized within a shared dependence on the public institutional framework of the state, which limits the scope of freedom. Thus 'in democratic and liberal institutional arrangements we may participate in collective forms of control over the control that is exercised over us as members of a polity', by deliberating and debating about these systems.[45]

Exit rights and communities of choice

Let us now return to the model of governance analysed in chapter 2, and the dynamic of cosmopolitan economic membership. The question to be tackled in this section is whether this model of governance and this system of membership can be reconciled with the principle of equality through access to the public sphere that has been identified as intrinsic to liberal democracy.

As we saw on pp. 51–5, the arguments for enhanced exit rights and 'voting with the feet' in the new model of public choice lie in the advantages of 'local and particular' collective goods, supplied to well-informed agents who choose a specific level of such provision and contribution rate when deciding to take up residence in a community of choice.[46] This allows efficiency gains from cost sharing with others who select the same combination of service and taxation levels, but also full consent to these, which might be represented in the form of a contract with existing members on entry. Thus joining a community of choice takes on many of the features of joining a club,[47] whose self-determination requires strict exclusion of those who do not pay the admission fee, for the sake of reserving benefits for members sharing costs and choosing optimum conditions. In these respects, membership of communities of choice is also highly compatible with commercial insurance (as in private health care plans or pension schemes).

One obvious consequence of this mechanism is that households with high incomes and few needs will try to group together, moving as far as possible from those with low incomes and many needs. 'The rich tend to want to be away from the poor, but the poor want to be in the same jurisdiction as the rich.'[48] Consent in contributions and over governance is therefore achieved through the selection effects of pricing (the costs of housing plus the tax rate), producing homogeneous memberships. 'There may well be a tendency for zoning on the part of high-income groups in order to exclude the poor.'[49]

Furthermore, the model relies almost entirely on allocations through the mobility of agents (exit strategies) rather than participation in discursive deliberation about improvements in particular collective services, or the overall quality of the shared life of a community (voice). The quasi-contractual relationship between members,[50] giving formal consent to the terms of membership on entry, and terminated simply on quitting residence and ceasing to pay dues, impoverishes the public sphere, and unbalances governance systems.

Finally, the logic of the model (efficient supply of collective goods to mobile agents by competing jurisdictions) justifies and enables the contracting out of public provision to private firms, who in turn compete to supply these at the lowest cost. Since these services simply enable the highest-quality infrastructure or consumption that members can afford, there are good reasons to seek the most efficient supplier through competitive tendering.

The model therefore undermines the fragile basis for equal membership under liberal democratic principles in the following three ways:

1 Exit rights and mobility promote communities and associations that are homogeneous and exclusive, and hence do not allow interactions and interdependencies to develop between the diversity of members of society as a whole. Instead they encourage segregations according to incomes and tastes, and reinforce divisions along the lines

of class and ethnicity. This allows mobility to become a means of competitive advantage, rather than an instrument of equal opportunity. 'A liberal egalitarian policy should try to make all cultural boundaries permeable so that individuals find ample opportunities to move out of their groups of origin and will also be accepted as full members when joining a different group.'[51]

As households cluster in homogeneous districts, it is not only that worse-off people are excluded from well-to-do neighbourhoods; poor districts become segregated on ethnic lines also, as was illustrated in the riots in Burnley, Oldham and Bradford in the UK in 2001.[52] This creation of ethnic communities of fate is partly a result of the increased reliance on kinship and friendship networks and on informal economic activity that impoverished lifestyles entail. In the black ghettos of US cities and the North African suburbs of French cities, similar concentrations of ethnic groups and social problems occur. But it is also a consequence of the transformation of urban space into areas of exclusive control, which residents patrol either with the discreet vigilantism of Neighbourhood Watch, or by the more violent methods associated with 'no-go areas', or the paramilitary groups in Northern Ireland.

2   Public services are institutional systems for pooling risks among diverse populations, based on compulsory contributions from members. They attempt to create common interests in good-quality education and health for all, as benefits of membership of society as a whole, and to equip all to participate on terms of equality as capable and healthy agents. These aims are defeated if those with most resources can use mobility to cluster around the most successful schools and hospitals, or to exit in favour of commercial systems.[53] These strategies gain individual advantage, instead of engaging with fellow members to

improve overall standards. The model empowers those able to use mobility for these ends, and disempowers the poorest and least mobile members.

Research shows that better-off households experience the shift from the postwar welfare state model to the one based on choice through mobility as a moral dilemma, and recognize that they are choosing between a version of equality among members, and one that allows their families positional advantage.[54] They see it as a dilemma over solidarity among citizens, or priority for family. In issues over basic rights of citizenship, liberal democratic institutions should avoid putting members in such a quandary.

3   The model loosens the connections between contributing to the common good through working in the public services, and sharing in the common good through using or benefiting from these services. In the liberal democratic version, being a teacher, a doctor, a nurse, a firefighter or a librarian was a form of service to the community, in which modest pay was balanced by high prestige and recognition for a key role in the public sphere. If these services are assessed purely in terms of their economic efficiency (value for taxpayers' money), and if they can be provided by companies from other regions or countries, under competitive contracts that may involve the periodic replacement of all staff in local facilities, then the ethos of both giving and receiving public services is transformed. It no longer makes sense to perceive the interactions within these services as definitive of the public sphere in which members communicate about common interests and issues, or deliberate about how to achieve common purposes.

As long as the main responsibility for funding human services (rather than environmental or infrastructural ones like the utilities, the post, the water supplies or transport systems) falls on government, a link between membership and receiving these is retained. But it is far more tenuous, because the relationships actually constructed within these institutions are not those between fellow members, but between 'providers' and 'customers' or 'consumers'.[55] The former are actively encouraged to see what they do as analogous to commercial services like banks and shops, and the latter to see themselves as knowledgeable buyers in a marketplace. As a UK policy document put it,

> Society has become more demanding. Consumers expect ever higher levels of service and better value for money.... Taxpayers want public agencies which meet their objectives efficiently.... Three trends highlight the rise of the demanding, sceptical, citizen-consumer. First, confidence in the institutions of government and politics has tumbled. Second, expectations of service quality and convenience have risen – as with the growth in 24-hour banking – but public services have failed to keep up with these developments; their duplication, inefficiency, and unnecessary complexity should not be tolerated. Third, as incomes rise, people prefer to own their own homes and investments.[56]

This model encourages an instrumental approach to both the supply and the use of public services. All outcomes must be measurable and costs specifiable; targets, quality control and accountability allow micro-management and budgetary constraint; programmes have definite aims and success or failure can be evaluated in quantified terms. 'Customers' and contributors know exactly what level of service to expect, and how to get redress if this is not delivered. This approach necessarily relegates qualitative aspects of interactions to the margins, and leaves little room for considerations of moral recognition or the exchange of value among members.

Nationality, redistribution and economic membership

The final aspect of cosmopolitan economic membership to be analysed in this chapter is its institutional solution to the central problems of all such systems – how to distinguish between those with full rights of membership, who participate as equal and autonomous agents, and those who do not, and what to do about populations involved in interactions and interdependencies within a society who are not full members. The model seems to offer a solution that is consistent with liberal democracy, by setting economic criteria for membership, and hence avoiding criteria that are based on gender or ethnic markers, or definitions of nationality. But this merely displaces the problems onto society and a residual polity, and requires new and coercive measures against those who do not qualify for full membership according to economic yardsticks.

In the 1990s, these problems have been clearest in Europe in relation to asylum seeking. Before the new policies to allow selective economic migration were begun in 2000, asylum was the main legal channel for entry during a whole decade.[57] Alarmed by their inability to regulate these inward flows, the EU and its member states created institutions (reception and detention centres, camps, tribunals and courts to 'fast-track' procedures, special and separate education and health facilities) that cordoned off asylum seekers from the public spheres of their societies, and visibly marked their non-membership during the processing of their claims.[58] These measures were intended to deter this form of entry, and to emphasize the status of asylum seekers as provisional entrants without the rights of membership, or the opportunities to participate as equals in social, economic or political interactions.

However, these new measures simultaneously drew fresh attention to all the other issues around membership status for all those who had entered earlier through channels for labour-market recruitment (guest workers) or family reunification, for those given refugee status or leave to remain, and for irregular migrants. Countries that had tried to avoid a 'politics of immigration' saw the sudden rise of populist movements, as in the Netherlands with the emergence of Pim Fortuyn's eponymous List, which survived the assassination of its leader in May 2002. Those that had contained anti-immigrant parties of the right, such as France, found their systems disrupted by the upsurge of support (as in Le Penism). Those (like the UK) with a longstanding politics of immigration and 'race' were forced to accommodate new forms of xenophobia, and the undermining of elaborate institutions for combating racism and enabling black and Asian citizens to participate as full members.

Both asylum and irregular migration give access to society, but not to full membership. New channels for economic migration raise new questions about transitions from the status of legal resident to that of citizen. Free movement of EU citizens exposes inconsistencies between member states like the UK, with restrictive immigration policies but relatively open access to full membership after a period of residence, and those like Germany, with more open borders but highly restrictive rules on naturalization. Liberal democratic principles condemn racist ideologies and political mobilizations, but are unable to give coherent accounts of how non-nationals qualify for admission to their societies, and how they then qualify for the transition from residence to full membership (and thus also to EU citizenship and rights to free movement).

The painful tensions between cosmopolitan economic membership and liberal democratic politics revealed by the rise of nationalist, racist and populist movements at the start of the present century demand active endorsement of the institutions and rules of equality and justice in European societies. The mass demonstrations in France after the first round of the presidential elections, and in the Netherlands after the assassination of Pim Fortuyn, seemed to provide such an answer. But the theoretical and practical challenges of defining and defending non-congruent rules of admission, of residence and of full membership are certain to recur in one form or another.

Yet at the same time, a closely related set of issues for liberal democracy has preoccupied both theorists and policy makers. These are questions about whether social rights of membership, and especially entitlements to income maintenance benefits, should be regarded as part of the institutional system that creates autonomous agents, capable of participation on a basis of equality, or whether they promote forms of dependency and free-riding that destroy the possibilities of such interactions.[59] If income transfers are not like education and health provision, if they do not lead to capabilities for responsible participation in the public sphere, then governments are justified in coercive measures towards populations who (like those who have entered the country without specific permission, either as asylum seekers or as irregular immigrants) require some process of determination, adjudication, categorization and training before they can be transformed into full members.

The new model of global governance does in fact construct just such a category, made up of nationals and non-nationals, who subsist outside formal systems of economic membership, though living within a society – as asylum seekers, irregular migrants, unemployed people, lone parents, and so on. The only characteristics these groups have in common are their dependence on the state for the means of survival, and their inability to supply the skills or pay the contributions required by businesses and communities of choice. From an economic standpoint, they therefore fall as costs upon those systems.[60] They cannot qualify for economic membership until they are reprocessed, with added value and the means to work and pay their dues. In order to reconcile their forms of membership with those of global governance and cosmopolitan economic institutions, states must therefore undertake these tasks.

This requires a radical redefinition of the rights and obligations of nationals, as well as severe restrictions of the liberties of these non-nationals. It implies that full membership for nationals is something to be earned, and for non-nationals to be entered via an economic gateway. But by (in effect) redefining all of them as suspended, potential or candidate members, this brings political and economic membership back into better alignment, and allows states to accommodate processes of globalization. It also requires arguments to legitimate regimes of compulsion (effectively forced labour and forced movement) and restrictions that could not be applied to free and equal citizens under liberal democratic principles.[61]

Such arguments have been developed in the USA,[62] along with measures to make public assistance payments conditional on work, training, marriage and parenting classes. They insist that economic inclusion, through formal labour market activity, is a necessary condition for the other forms of inclusion that comprise full membership. Hence an application for income support from the revenues collected by government from economically independent, hardworking taxpayers is morally equivalent to arriving in a country without means of support, a job or a work permit. Claimants of public assistance are as justifi-ably required to undertake these programmes, as prepara-tions for and demonstrations of their willingness to reassume the responsibilities of full membership, as would-be immigrants (such as asylum seekers) are to be required to spend a period under containment in special centres, while the grounds for their applications are assessed.

Liberal democratic theorists in the UK and in Europe are deeply divided about the validity of such arguments[63] – both for conditions and compulsion around redistribu-tive benefits, and over the restriction of the liberty of asylum seekers.[64] But modified regimes of this kind have been adopted in almost all European countries, even though it is only in the UK that government has tried to define a new 'social contract' with benefit claimants, spelling out the obligations on them in return for receiving assistance[65] as well as 'fairer, faster and firmer' terms for admitting immigrants.[66] The important point is that econ-omic status determines whether nationals have basic free-doms (against coercive interventions by state agents), and economic gateways allow residence and access to society by non-nationals (who would be turned away or locked up if they tried to enter through other channels). In this sense, nationals without the means of subsistence lack the rights of full members, and non-nationals in the same predicament cannot enter that society as free agents.

Thus nationality becomes a less important determinant of certain fundamental rights than economic membership. Of course, citizenship status still confers political rights, and in this sense is the only form of full membership. But in some ways non-national residents who are economically independent are more fully members of these societies than economically dependent nationals are; and both nationals and non-nationals who cannot achieve economic independence are in somewhat similar forms of reduced, provisional, suspended or conditional membership. It is employers (and especially transnational corporations) who effectively determine who are to be admitted as economic recruits from abroad, and who are needed as employees from national populations; hence they confer economic independence, and its membership status.

This shift replaces morally arbitrary systems of national membership that excluded non-nationals because they were not born into a political community of fate, or not descended from its citizens, by systems that select or admit individuals from all over the world for their assets or potential contributions, but relegate others (both nationals and non-nationals) who lack such assets, or are not so selected. In the UK, the work permits system is extremely responsive to the needs of large employers, and grants them virtual exemption from having to recruit from the home population. This is consistent with liberal democratic principles of non-discriminatory equal global opportunity, but it leaves the vast majority of the world's population, and a considerable minority of the citizens of First World countries, without basic rights to subsistence from their governments.

Conclusions

Without explicitly privileging national political membership over other principles, liberal democratic theory and practice tended to do so in the second half of the twentieth century. This was partly by omission; theories of justice, such as Rawls's[67] or Sen's,[68] and theories of equality, such as Dworkin's[69] or Cohen's,[70] did not deal in boundary questions, or say how individuals were admitted to or excluded from membership. It was also partly by design, because the rights of membership, which supplied access to equality and justice, were the prerogative of citizens, and citizenship was primarily a political concept, and implied belonging to a nation state, with territorial sovereignty in a system of similar states. Finally, claims of independence and equality of status by emerging former colonial peoples were linked to nationality and nation states, so global justice seemed to demand that such societies were treated in the same ways, as self-determining systems of membership like First World states. In this chapter we have shown how other principles of equality and justice have been analysed in liberal democratic theory as relationships between members, with the unstated assumption that they were citizens of such political communities.

These assumptions were challenged by the presence of non-national populations, with diverse cultures and political commitments; by the hostile reactions of some nationals to these fellow members of their societies; by issues about access to citizenship status; and by pressure, especially in the 1990s, for admission by migrants from far-distant countries without historical links. Although many of these challenges stemmed from integration of the world's economy, globalization seemed to pose new issues of equality and justice, without offering new solutions. Transnational investment, production and trade all increased mobility for business purposes, and involved accelerated movement of others – students, tourists, shoppers – across national borders, affording greater opportunities for irregular migration. International conventions on humanitarian protection of asylum seekers were unspecific about national obligations, and appeared to facilitate movements of populations in search of political freedoms, and perhaps of economic opportunities, rather than from persecution (narrowly defined).

The model of global governance set out in chapter 2 demands extensive modifications of the rights given to citizens, and the powers of national political communities, in order to facilitate the further integration of the world economy, including opening up state infrastructures and public services to competition from foreign firms. This requires the development of systems of cosmopolitan economic membership that allow global economic agents rights of residence, and powers to recruit staff worldwide. All these developments would be facilitated by extensions of the principles discussed in this chapter, for the devolution of jurisdiction over collective services, the enhanced mobility of well-informed agents, and the commercialization of much public provision. But these principles seriously undermine the notion of a public sphere in a political community, in which citizens interact as equal members. Hence something has to give. Either liberal democracy tries to preserve its model of political membership through rights giving equal capabilities of autonomous participation, and common interests in the goods of the public sphere, without being able to provide coherent principles for admission to such a community under conditions of globalization; or it adopts economic criteria for admissions and exclusions, which allow non-nationals greater access, and abate some forms of ethnic and cultural discrimination, but considerably reduce the substantial rights of citizenship, and especially those of the poor, and allow harsh treatment of those non-nationals who seek entry without meeting the criteria for economic inclusion.

The latter model would not abolish distinctions between the rights and opportunities of nationals and non-nationals, or the territorial definition of boundaries of membership through nation states. Citizenship would still be an important status, allowing rights to enter into

collective decisions about all the state's main legal principles, including immigration rules. In this sense, those
without full political membership, however rich and influential in their spheres, would still have a more precarious,
marginal status than citizens. The upsurge of nationalism
and racism in European politics at the start of this century
showed that this latent precariousness could suddenly
become overt and manifest. But the residual role of the
state in everyday issues of economic and social life, and
the narrow range of choices open to national governments,
create a paradox. Although nationality and citizenship are
still the keys to collective power in the basic structures of
liberal democratic politics, and in determining who has
access to this dimension of membership, politics itself is a
far less powerful determinant of the institutional systems
and economic outcomes of interactions in national communities. And the public life that is the substance of
citizenship, in which citizens of all classes, all ethnic
groups and both genders meet as equals, to deliberate
upon, decide, create and inhabit a sphere of common
interest in the common good, shrinks to a small part of
society's exchanges, experienced as a cost rather than a
benefit of membership.

As populations are sorted into residential districts with
homogeneous populations, poor and disadvantaged people, both nationals and non-nationals, group together in
ethnic huddles within deprived communities of fate. Not
only are the concentrations of social problems – violence,
theft, drug abuse, family fragmentation – generated by
such communities enormously costly for their members;
they fall as high costs upon the residents of communities
of choice. Poor people are perceived as burdens and
threats when they are encountered, and contacts lead to
resentment and fear. This justifies an enforcement ethos
in all social programmes, with an emphasis on combating

abuse and fraud, and protecting taxpayers' interests.[71] Prison populations expand, and public interactions become tense and stressful.

These features of societies (like the USA and UK) that have gone furthest down the road prescribed by the new model allow the suspension of the liberties of all who become dependent on the state to be justified. Poverty itself becomes an indicator of a whole range of other social problems, and legitimates interventions that impose a discipline of work and order. Provision through public programmes is surrounded by conditions and rules that tie recipients to the performance of approved tasks, the occupation of required roles, or habitation of controlled spaces. In order to receive assistance, claimants must be willing to accept employment, training, treatment or regimes of residential resocialization. Liberal democracy compromises its principles of equality and freedom to protect the property rights of rich and mobile people.

In the final chapter we will investigate whether this is a necessary price to pay for the free transnational movement of a cosmopolitan elite, or whether the benefits of more open borders could be more widely spread without infringements of equality and justice among citizens.

5

Global Equality and Justice

Globalization is transforming economic and social relations – but into what? Some of the most radical critics of international capitalism see in its creative destruction the possibilities for an ethical transformation. There might be a window of opportunity for the emergence of a post-capitalist order of sustainable development, environmental conservation and social justice.

Justice is concerned with the way in which social institutions distribute fundamental rights, duties and the advantages from social co-operation.[1] This in turn is part of a 'vision of society', and of the aims and purposes of such co-operation.[2] The ideal of a society in which individuals contribute voluntarily, with their full potential, to activities that meet the needs of all is shared by many versions in which institutions for justice allow society's members to agree common purposes, but leave them enough freedom to pursue their own. Utopian ideas from the early nineteenth[3] and early twentieth[4] centuries are being re-examined in the face of challenges to nation states, gross inequalities in global distributions, and the end of the bipolar order of the Cold War period.[5]

This book has set out to restate the issues for theory of equality and justice in terms appropriate for the twenty-first century. The most influential of these theories in the previous fifty years were derived from 'thought experiments' in which pre-social, pre-economic and pre-political beings, confined to ante-chambers[6] or desert islands[7] to design the institutions for their lives together, debated principles under which they would compete for roles and resources.

These analytical devices appealed to the notion of a social contract in which individuals formed a political community and decided on its basic structure – the tradition of Hobbes, Locke and Rousseau. As we argue in this chapter, this approach still has much to offer to the analysis of equality and justice, but it can no longer ignore the issues of mobility and membership that are ruled out by imagining societies with no boundaries, no insiders and outsiders, and no problems of entry and exit.[8]

These omissions are clearest in the work of John Rawls. As recently as 1993, in his *Political Liberalism*, he justified the assumption that, for purposes of justice, in the 'original position' membership of a society is fixed.[9] 'Political society is closed: we come to be within it and we do not, and indeed cannot, enter or leave it voluntarily.'[10] It is only in his last book, *The Law of Peoples* (1999), that Rawls deals in issues concerning the boundaries of political communities, and then from a perspective of liberal nationalism. The role of a 'people's government' (a state) is to take responsibility for territory and the size of population.[11] Such agents 'cannot make up for their irresponsibility in caring for their land and its natural resources by conquest in war or by migrating into other people's territory without their consent'.[12] In a footnote to this, Rawls endorses Walzer's view that an absence of immigration controls would lead to internal restrictions of movement and closure of organizations.[13]

What our analysis has attempted to show is that there are no conceivable rules of equality and justice that can transcend all questions of boundaries, inclusion and exclusion. This is because competition for roles and resources necessarily creates memberships, insiders and outsiders. Since human beings are intrinsically footloose and rivalrous, any institutions that attempt to address these principles cannot aim simply for stability and harmony. Regimes for equality and justice must take account of people's propensity to disagree about how to achieve these goals, to quarrel about the good way of life, and to leave in search of better. Rights to such recriminations and exits are not regrettable allowances for avoidable breakdowns of co-operation on terms of fairness; they are essential parts of what we mean by equality and justice.

These issues arise in all forms of membership groups, and in all kinds of societies. Families are systems for dealing with (among other things) the dependence of small children and frail elderly people upon those of an age to be both mobile and productively active. Principles of equality and justice in families were traditionally based on the idea that women were genetically less footloose and rivalrous than men, better suited to meeting the dependency needs of children and old people, and therefore naturally equipped for sedentary caring. Moral and legal rules therefore restrained the scope for men's mobility, and created obligations towards women and children. But once women are seen as potentially just as footloose and rivalrous as men, all these rules have to be rewritten to allow them equal rights of access to competition in productive activity, and to mobility and exit in all other spheres.[14]

Because – as Hobbes pointed out – human beings are intrinsically weak and vulnerable as well as quarrelsome and itinerant, institutions are required to protect them, as well as to allow them scope for rivalry and roaming. What this book has sought to do is draw attention to the equal vulnerability of sedentary and migrant populations under conditions of globalization. The institutional regimes for equality and justice created in the second half of the twentieth century were designed to cater for free mobility of nationals within societies, and allow entry to and exit from all these societies' internal organizations for membership, in ways that took account of their vulnerabilities and needs for protection. Economies conceived as national oligopolies of large firms and oligopsonies of large trade unions, societies made up of male breadwinners and their dependants (women, children, older people), and polities supposedly composed of stable populations of culturally and ethnically homogeneous citizens were the elements of such national institutional arrangements. Non-nationals did not come into the reckoning.[15]

Globalization has created new forms of vulnerability, as well as new sources of wealth and power. It has allowed the development of new kinds of transnational economic membership, as well as weakening the protections of social citizenship. We have shown that the accelerated movement across borders of skilled and resourceful nomads, through wealthy and powerful corporations, has led to transformations under which some persecuted or destitute individuals from strife-torn and disrupted communities take flight, while others in prosperous societies remain sedentary in pockets of deprivation. States in turn have developed institutions for confining most of the former in concentration camps (by any other name), and coercing the latter into forced labour (by any other name) for the interests of the winners in these processes. Instead of protecting the most vulnerable migrants and sedentary people, new institutional regimes take away rights from these groups that are given to all other members.

In this chapter, we argue that equality and justice demand a balance of rights for migratory and sedentary lifestyles. People need opportunities and protections, whether they roam abroad or remain in stable communities. Institutions should be designed to allow them to travel, and to engage with others, as equal and autonomous agents. But they should also allow membership groups to distribute roles and resources according to principles of justice. Market institutions maximize mobility, but not equality among participants; political institutions organize membership, but not necessarily justice between members, or fair access for non-members. Postwar institutions organized markets within systems of political membership; global institutions reorganize states as infrastructures for economic activity.

If all people are morally equal, and hence all should have equal access to membership systems, then there is only one large human community, embracing the whole world's population. The basic insight of globalism is that only this political community (whatever its institutional forms) has a right to impose non-contractual binding arrangements on constituent organizations. This insight is implicit in the notion of human rights, and in the ethical assertion that the USA is not justified in imposing 'regime changes' without the support of the United Nations.

This moral universalism demands that primary social goods are distributed among the world's population as a whole. So far, we have explored the relevance of organizational boundaries for issues of equality and justice, by showing that nationalism, globalism, federalism and liberal democracy are all incomplete and internally incoherent. None can, on its own, either justify, or justify the abolition of, territorial boundaries or political memberships. We now turn to the logically separate task of arguing that rights to income are the features of a 'basic structure' of social relations, combining all four perspectives, which can be most equitably and efficiently distributed as the basis of substantial equality. We take the basic income proposal as the most promising institutional form for such distributions and illustrate the remaining dilemmas for its advocates once boundary issues are taken into account.

The challenge that we take up in this chapter is to analyse the institutions that might balance freedom and mobility with protection, recognition[16] and membership. So far we have focused on the shortcomings of nationalism, globalism and federalism, and the incoherences of liberal democracy. But we have also identified elements in all of them that might contribute to a balanced set of social arrangements that fulfils many of the ideals of voluntary co-operation, while allowing change, including access by newcomers with new ideas.

States as membership systems

Individual adult human beings are more or less equally mobile, and more or less equally vulnerable;[17] it costs about the same to fence any one of them in or out, and to feed or kill any one. In liberal democratic theory, they are morally equal, so it is impossible to give moral reasons for selecting some for and excluding others from membership or physical survival. The efficiency of productive economic activity requires mobility, and mobility requires a basic level of health and welfare to sustain it. Therefore logically people should be free to move, to choose where to live and work, in order to sustain themselves. They should also have access to the means of survival as they do so. These principles apply to the internal organization of states as economies and societies, and there are no persuasive reasons why they should not apply to the whole world as an integrated economic system. In so far as societies are economies, they should therefore be as open as possible, and in so far as states organize societies as economies in a particular territory, they should provide institutions to facilitate openness.

But many human needs can be met only in associations, as systems of recognition, reciprocity, nurturing, education, care, reproduction, intimacy, cultural exchange and recreation. Such systems run on common interests in sharing and redistribution among members, through collective institutions that define boundaries of inclusion and exclusion. To be democratic and self-determining, they must therefore distinguish between rights and responsibilities of their memberships, and rules for dealing with outsiders.

Neither societies nor polities as 'communities' are associations of this kind. One fallacy of communitarianism is to attribute to societies and polities all the characteristics of families and voluntary associations, and claim that they therefore have rights of exclusion, and powers to impose responsibilities, of these kinds.[18] Another is that all moral rules and systems derive from closed membership groups, and that therefore no moral duties are owed to non-members.[19] Neither of these claims is valid, since societies must constantly accommodate flows of population, both in and out, and political communities are mainly consequences of where people are born, and not whom they have chosen to share their lives with.[20]

However, states are both political communities and systems of social reproduction, as well as frameworks for economic activity. They are therefore concerned with creating common interests in shared facilities for a public life among their members, as well as open systems allowing the most efficient allocation of skills and productive resources. Although they cannot extrapolate from voluntary associations to justify coercive exclusions of outsiders, or compulsory obligations to perform forced labour for the common good, they do have duties to protect the activities and associations that make up these systems, and to create ones of their own to overcome collective action problems between them.

So states are a mixture of systems, and their institutions regulate polities, societies and economies, all of which have their own membership systems. Societies can function well as open systems; the example of cosmopolitan global cities (see pp. 103–4) shows how very diverse yet concentrated networks may allow intensive interactions within the same social space. Political membership gives rise to collective decisions over the rules for such interactions, by democratic processes, but it need not be seen as the dominant element in them. In liberal democratic systems, political participation is not obligatory. This is the fallacy of civic republicanism, which sees the boundaries of a society as justified by the requirements of active citizenship.[21] This not only excludes non-nationals from society; it excludes social issues from the mainstream concerns of politics.[22]

The key questions therefore are how states can provide open access to their economies, while protecting the individual vulnerabilities of their populations, and promoting the common interests that sustain their associational and political membership systems. For the sake of equality and justice, they cannot simply reinforce either of these processes, but must genuinely mediate between them, according to these principles. If they do no more than endorse or accentuate the outcomes of market systems, they will constantly give advantages to individuals and organizations with accumulations of wealth or skills. If they merely strengthen and reinforce associational systems, including their own national communities, they will constantly exclude the claims of outsiders, whether from the vulnerable unorganized national population, from settled ethnic minorities, or from other countries.

The institutional systems established by states in the second half of the twentieth century were exclusive of women, in the ways that they reinforced traditional family power and dependency relations; exclusive of people with disabilities and handicaps, in confining them to homes and hospitals; exclusive of ethnic minorities, in denying them the full status of citizenship; and exclusive of non-nationals in protecting nationals' jobs and wages from competition by foreigners. They sought equality and justice mainly in terms of protections and redistributions in the economic sphere, by regulating labour markets and transferring income between groups of male employees and their families within national economies. They had no ways of taking account of the interests of those outside their boundaries; criteria of efficiency and equity were derived solely from the welfare of national populations.[23]

The new model regimes promoted by international organizations at the start of this century reverse these priorities. Their openness, their responsiveness to financial markets, the access they give to transnational corporations, and the scope for economic membership systems all embrace global market processes, and endorse their outcomes. This has direct consequences for all kinds of associational systems. Families are required to provide more members for the labour market in order to maintain their living standards, so they must adapt the way they care for children and older relatives.[24] Associations of all kinds must adopt commercial principles of accounting, and demonstrate their value in economic terms to their members. They must become self-financing, and must charge members economic contributions for their collective facilities.[25] Even the intimate ties of informal membership systems are reconceptualized as 'social capital'.

Individuals and associations must acquire property hold-ings, and see their assets as stores of wealth, or sources of income.[26] States must transform their public infrastruc-tures and social services in line with these requirements.

Above all, as we showed in chapter 4, states are under pressure from international organizations to cut back those protections for their populations that shelter them from competition, and to supply active, adaptable and well-motivated workers for their labour markets. Hence they are driven into a round of reducing public benefits and labour-market standards, and tightening conditions of eligibility for what is available. The only ways in which they can legitimately protect the living standards of their populations in such regimes are by closing borders to all those who are not recruited by employers based inside their territory, and confining within quasi-prisons those who present themselves as asylum seekers.

But these regimes also link membership to economic contribution and performance, and hence to 'civic com-petence' or 'responsible citizenship'. The new model's version of economic membership and the Third Way's emphasis on work obligations are complementary in these respects. In the next section, we argue that there are indications that politicians and policy makers are aware of the ways that these regimes violate principles of equality and justice, and that these give some clues about the directions in which they might be reformed in the name of these principles.

Rights that promote equal autonomy

The ethical justification of the substantial rights of citizen-ship in postwar welfare states was that they enabled members to participate as equals in the economy and in

the associations of civil society. They also included them
as equal members of the political community, by virtue of
the fact that all were bearers of these rights. 'Democracy
implies an equal status of membership in a polity, and
liberalism demands that every person subjected to political
power ought to enjoy liberties and rights which secure . . .
autonomy in relation to that power.'[27] In the shared
institutional frameworks supplied by these states, rights
protected and legitimated the identities, needs and
interests of members in their interactions in every sphere.
These rights were always backed by a strong norm of
juridical equality, because liberal democratic governments
were obliged to seek legitimacy by treating citizens with
equal concern, and as equals.[28]

Hence the justification for substantial rights was based
on the requirement of these societies for members capable
of making their own choices and being responsible for
their actions, and on the demand that they could produce
political communities capable of resolving conflicts and
upholding collective decisions.[29] 'Substantial citizenship
could be defined as rights to those capabilities that are
required for autonomous agency in the public sphere of
civil society and for equal membership in the polity.'[30] For
example, the right to education could be seen as an
entitlement of adults to have their mental and physical
endowments formed into capabilities[31] of effective participation in the economy, in associations, and in the political
system.[32] The right to health care lay in the entitlement to
have such capabilities restored when they were jeopard-
ized by illness, to which all members are more or less
equally vulnerable. And the right to security of income
rested on the entitlement to protection from harm and
loss during the processes of moving and choosing within
labour markets that require movement and choice.[33] In
this sense, income security could be seen as like the right

to travel within society without being attacked;[34] it gave a capability in labour markets similar to that provided by law and order in wider society.

In the new model of governance promoted by global organizations, these rights are criticized as passive entitlements, that can simply be used as protections for a life of sedentary dependency, without responsibility to other members.[35] Hence all substantial rights should be given in regimes of activation, which emphasize the duty to contribute to society, to be independent, and not to fall as a cost on fellow citizens.[36] In this view, education and health care should be specifically and overtly linked to labour-market capabilities, and the regimes that surround them point unambiguously towards economic participation as the goal of provision. Above all, income maintenance should be conditional, and regulations strictly enforced, because its moral justification lies in capabilities to adapt and earn, not to live at the expense of the community. Activation regimes are justified because they make this explicit;[37] workfare is not forced labour, but the provision of opportunities for the exercise of responsible autonomy.[38]

The countries that have gone furthest in putting these policies into practice (the USA and the UK) have recognized that they contain the potential for injustice through the exercise of state power against a vulnerable minority on behalf of an advantaged majority. They attempt to protect the rights of claimants in three ways. The first is to introduce tests of 'genuine need' into income maintenance systems, so that those who can prove that they have made unsuccessful efforts to get work, or are physically incapable of doing the work that is available, can get payments.[39] The second is to use tax credits to supplement the wages of those with few skills, and hence low earning power. And the third is by retaining minimum wages, albeit at low levels. All these are supposed to give added justifications for activation regimes, by preventing unjust coercion by the authorities, and unjust exploitation by employers.

These concessions go only part way to recognizing the moral arguments against more conditionality and tougher enforcement. Rights to education, health and income security rest on the value of autonomy and choice among equal citizens, and this extends to every sphere of society. Civil and political rights are given to all citizens, regardless of their merits or deserts.[40] Substantial rights promote participation and membership of society as a whole, and not only the labour market. 'The basic requirement of political justice is to provide all members of society with a comprehensive bundle of citizenship rights that takes into account their different social positions and group affiliations but enables them to see themselves as equal individual members of the polity.'[41] This extends to the associational life of the community, to its cultural activities, and to sustaining political as well as economic activism. It includes family life, and the care of children and older people. Substantial rights create the possibility of choice and autonomy in all these roles,[42] enable the participants in all of them to negotiate their responsibilities to each other as equals, and allow individuals to balance the contributions they make to each sphere of activity. In order to remain neutral between various conceptions of the good life, and promote responsible autonomy, the state should uphold the right to withdraw from active participation in any of these spheres, or all of them.

So it is not enough to protect the rights of those who are sick or disabled not to be coerced to work or left destitute; or to give income supplements through tax credits to those with low earnings; or to regulate minimum wages. Income maintenance provision should support and promote all forms of participation in society, and do so on terms that sustain interactions between autonomous agents, who enter their relationships as equals. This implies that support should either be linked to *any* form of social activity, paid or unpaid (a 'participation income'[43]); or – if that proved far too costly and cumbersome to test and administer – that it should be unconditional (a 'basic income'[44]). Although the new model adopted in the USA and the UK seems to point in the opposite direction, towards greater conditionality, tougher enforcement, and narrower entitlement criteria, the moral arguments for exceptions, for tax credits and for minimum wages all indicate underlying rights to equal autonomy that demand recognition.

Tax and benefits systems are redistributions for the sake of justice between members. We have strongly criticized the way in which they have been turned into instruments for enforcing work obligations on citizens under the new model pioneered in the USA and the UK. From an ethical standpoint, income maintenance payments represent the value of the individual to the political community. In a polity that values each member equally, there are therefore strong reasons to support the principle of an equal and unconditional allowance (either a payment or a tax credit) for each individual member – a basic income, or social dividend.[45] The former would be given at regular intervals (weekly or monthly); alternatively, the latter would be a capital grant, or an allocation of land (which might be most appropriate in a developing country). Which principles of redistribution would govern such a system, and how might they be influenced by the pattern of membership systems and political communities?

We use the basic income proposal as a focus for evaluating the contributions of nationalism, globalism and federalism to an ethically justifiable version of a world order.

Its advocates argue that the principle of basic income (or something like it) is the best way of creating a measure of social justice, substantial equality and autonomy (as opposed to procedural justice, juridical equality and mere freedom) under the circumstances of the present-day globalized economy. But they seldom discuss the issues raised by agents moving between basic income jurisdictions, variations in the rates of basic income between jurisdictions, or the appropriate level of the authority that will gather taxes and distribute basic incomes. Thus the proposal provides an opportunity to examine how nationalist, globalist and federalist theories of membership deal with these questions.

Universal human rights or national citizenship rights?

In the previous section, we argued that individuals should be free to choose where to live and work, and that if they move, they should do so as bearers of substantial rights to those benefits and services that they need in order to participate as equal and autonomous members in whichever societies they join. One approach to the design of institutions for achieving these goals is to extend the features of citizenship first developed in the era of welfare states, to allow individuals to become itinerant workers, transnational activists, members of international kinship chains or faith communities, and global nomads. Although the nationalist perspective is inordinately anxious that too many of them might become international 'welfare regime-shoppers', it has provided, in citizenship, a conception of equality and social justice that is capable of extension in many such ways, systematically explored in the work of Rainer Bauböck.[46]

Globalism supplies the principal alternative to this approach – human rights. If the world is a single moral community, and all human beings are entitled to the rights identified above, then the only collective authority to guarantee these, and enforce compliance with them by all constituent organizations, including those at the level of nation states, is a global one. Setting aside for a moment the vast problem of aggregating the votes of the world's population to give such an authority democratic legitimacy, a system of international governance could reflect the *constitutional* basis of the global order, as defined by contractarians through such devices as the veil of ignorance and the original position. The parties to Rawls's social contract would be representatives of the whole world's population, and of all societies, rather than his closed 'society'.

The theory of fiscal federalism, in turn, provides important insights into how a global structure's levels of collective decision making might be integrated. The case for decentralization in the supply of collective goods – the efficiency gains through economic clubs that straddle territorial boundaries, and free mobility between jurisdictions with authority over bundles of infrastructural goods – entrusts all responsibility for income distribution and environmental protection to the highest possible level of authority.[47] Given the propensities of decentralization of this kind to select in ways that polarize populations between good-quality and shoddy social services, and between luxurious and sordid districts, and the more general dangers of income inequality and environmental degradation of a 'race to the bottom' between lower-level authorities, there is a strong case for those responsibilities to be exercised through a system of international governance.

If the basic income approach to income distribution

can deliver a new version of equality and autonomy, it makes sense that the whole world's population should get a uniform global basic income (GBI) from such a body; but each of them should be supplied with health, education and other social services through systems of overlapping clubs, regulated at the regional or national level, and have access to infrastructural goods, provided through local jurisdictions, under similar forms of regulation. Federalism gives an economic rationale for this balance between the different levels of governance, and the ethical principles of social justice the case for constitutional rights to adequate income and mobility rights between all membership systems.

We have identified many features of the globalization process that tend in the direction of such an institutional design. There is an integrated system of global governance, whose present purpose is to make constituent political communities accountable to financial markets. It would be a total reversal of this hierarchy of power and authority to make financial companies and business corporations accountable to international governance instead, and to impose taxes (like the proposed 'Tobin tax' on speculative currency transactions[48]) to fund a GBI. Many have doubted whether such ideas could be implemented.[49] But we should recall that globalization itself involved a similar reversal in the hierarchy of power, from national systems of regulation (welfare states) to the international market order (see pp. 7–9).

Alternatively, while recognizing that this might well be the fairest and most desirable endpoint of the ethical transformation of social relations worldwide, another pathway would be the extension of citizenship rights to free movement, and a national basic income (NBI). This would be set at the highest level affordable by each national government, and would therefore vary between states. The global principle of basic income would require the authoritative endorsement of the international governance system, which might supplement the NBI of the poorest member states; but the basis for (unequal) basic incomes would still be citizenship. People who moved abroad would (initially at least) get their NBI from their original country of citizenship (see pp. 143–9 below).

The arguments for this approach rest on the priority for democratic principles of collective authority, the balance between exit and voice rights, the value of plurality and diversity of political communities, and impartiality between nomadic and sedentary lifestyles. Whereas the case for a GBI uses the economic rationale of fiscal federalism, that for an NBI asserts these ethical principles. It therefore seeks to justify the continuing priority for national systems of membership (based on common interests between citizens) and the international order of nation states.

In this perspective, democratic practices are intrinsically valuable, and all membership systems lose legitimacy to the extent that they fail to nurture democratic participation. National political communities have been more successful in sustaining institutions for democracy than have larger bodies, such as the EU or the United Nations. Furthermore, for democratic voice to have any substantial effectiveness, political participation must be able to shape institutions, as well as outcomes within them. Only through a variety of democratic processes, in a plurality of vibrant political communities, can democratic politics be real and engaging. Citizenship is an active role, concerned with shaping polities, and cultivating civic virtues.[50] The globalist governance envisaged in a GBI risks appearing to be an attempt to impose a standard institutional design without reference to the national political traditions that sustain democracy.

To balance rights of exit and voice, and promote common interests, solidarity and loyalty, the national basis for the NBI is therefore important. Especially since other social services would be supplied through transnational clubs, and local authorities would continue to be significant membership systems, the enhanced mobility of the new order needs to be offset by institutions voted in democratic and solidaristic political traditions, and susceptible to the influence of participant members. Even the modest levels of the NBIs available to the populations of poor countries would provide them with the means for subsistence, and allow the 98 per cent who still live in their countries of citizenship worldwide to remain there, rather than having to resort to nomadism to sustain their lives.

The difficult questions for the NBI approach concern the justice of the relationships between citizens and non-citizens, nomadic and sedentary populations, that they would allow. Freedom of movement across borders, and a 'portable' NBI, would enable people from poor countries with a modest allowance to enter rich ones, and people from rich countries with more generous allowances to enter poor ones. If income distribution systems become the main instruments for social justice worldwide, then this would create a serious anomaly. Within each state, citizens and non-citizens would interact on terms that were by definition unjust, since they would have different rates of basic income. It would also give much greater significance to procedures for naturalization, through which new entrants qualified for citizenship, and hence for the NBI of the receiving country (see below, pp. 144–5). A universal GBI, with the same level for all, would avoid these problems, but would of course be paid at a far lower rate, insufficient for decent subsistence in developed economies.

One issue for the NBI approach would be impartiality between mobile and sedentary lifestyles. Some would argue that unconditional citizenship-based allowances would favour sedentary agents unduly, and be a kind of subsidy for immobility (rather as social insurance benefits are in present-day Germany). The counter-argument is that public transport systems are all, in effect, heavily subsidized in First World countries, because mobile agents do not pay the full costs of their journeys. They involve large transfers from sedentary citizens to national and non-national nomads. Hence basic incomes for citizens would compensate for such hidden subsidies for mobility and migration.

The arguments for NBI attempt to reconcile democratic membership with free mobility by maintaining the boundaries of national political communities. The universal principle of equality insists that all individuals are entitled to leave a state, first provisionally and temporarily, then (eventually) by renouncing their citizenship. Rights of exit, like rights of entry, imply a plurality of states,[51] each with different bundles of substantial rights, and different opportunities to take part in collective decisions, within different institutional structures, reflecting different interpretations of equality and justice. The problems for basic income schemes of movement between memberships of such systems will be analysed in the next section.

Admission to and renunciation of citizenship

One of the foremost advocates of the extension of rights of citizenship to those moving across borders and entering states is Rainer Bauböck. Although he does not specifically advocate an NBI, he indicates his general approval of the principle it embodies.[52] His analysis of admission to and renunciation of citizenship is therefore of relevance to the evaluation of this proposal.

Not all people who enter a country are applicants for citizenship. People come on business visits, as tourists, as diplomats, or to buy a holiday home. Global nomads come to work, but not to settle. So the process of applying for citizenship is logically separate from entry. Whereas all countries have rules on admission to citizenship through birth or descent, which involve *automatic* membership of a political community of fate, the admission of adults to citizenship implies not only consent, but also a positive choice, which cannot be expressed simply by entering territory.[53] So it is consistent with universal principles of equality to make rules about how those who freely enter a country exercise options to become full members through naturalization.[54]

Bauböck argues (following Locke[55]) that the decision to naturalize involves a kind of commitment.[56] Naturalization is quite a different process from being born into a liberal democratic state, being educated within its norms, and learning to participate in it through everyday life and public affairs.[57] Hence naturalization is a kind of 'resocialization', and takes time; it can be facilitated by government policies and provision of language classes and other forms of education. This justifies imposing a period of waiting, from taking up residence on joining a society, to being eligible to exercise an option of admission to citizenship.[58]

This choice over citizenship concerns access to a particular status within such a political community. Citizenship is about 'making political rule in territorially bounded states democratic by giving equal liberties and rights to those who are subjected to this rule and who have a stake in the common good of this society'.[59] So entry into a society, as a worker or a resident, is a step towards such membership, but not a direct claim to it. Equally, leaving to live or work abroad is not a renunciation of citizenship. Therefore there are still important questions to be answered about which rights and responsibilities are appropriate for members of a society who are not (yet) citizens, and for citizens who are not currently members of that society.

Within the European Union, citizens of member states have free movement between these states, and some political rights within these also; but third-country nationals have no such rights, even where (as in Germany) many of them were born in their states of residence.[60] Finally, asylum seekers are contained under conditions that would be abuses of civil and social rights if they were applied to citizens of any member state. To establish free movement of citizens, the governments of member states were required to set up reciprocal voting arrangements, and community funds for redistributing resources from the rich north to the poor south (the Common Agricultural Policy and the Structural and Cohesion Funds).[61]

Bauböck argues strongly for citizenship rights to be extended to all members of societies, and also for the extension of such rights to national populations living outside territorial boundaries.[62] The inclusivity of democratic conceptions of membership and the priority for equality under liberalism demand the former; but migration also extends the reach of such rights beyond nation states, which demands the latter. 'In this way, democratic citizenship questions the existing forms of segmentation, extends the space of politically organized society and creates a complex map of overlapping memberships.'[63] Political communities cannot be confined within state boundaries, and multiple and interstate citizenships become necessary, as the universalized rights of national membership are extended to a transnational level.[64] States are formidable systems for social control over society, and therefore all members of society require the full set of citizenship rights to live on equal terms with others.[65] The fact that citizenship is tied to particular places and populations does not make it less universal, or less encompassing of the whole world's population, since the state is now the universal political organization of membership.[66] 'And in this context, not every substantive account of justice is a local one, contrary to what communitarians want to make us believe.'[67]

What is most important for justice is that rights actually protect against all new forms of inequality, power and control;[68] there is no point in extending rights to include all those living within societies, or those travelling and working outside them, unless these actually shield their vulnerabilities, cover them against risks, and enable them to participate in the relevant dimensions of activity. The key questions are therefore which non-nationals are most vulnerable to which kinds of domination or exploitation, and which citizens are exposed to new risks under the new global order.

The answer to the first question is that asylum seekers are the most unprotected non-nationals, since they are quite likely to be effectively stateless, and exposed to coercive authority and loss of liberty within the societies where they seek refuge. But free movement would allow them to enter such societies, to live there legally, and to work, to secure their survival. Hence they would have the same rights as other migrants, which would be a great improvement on their present situation.

The answer to the second is that people with few skills, living in deprived communities of fate, or depressed districts or regions, are the groups that are exposed to new risks under the new order. They have lost rights, compared with such groups in postwar welfare state regimes, and they suffer new disadvantages, because they lack the property rights, human and social capital available to mainstream citizens, and experience the hazards and jeopardies of living in areas of concentrated social problems.

The purpose of the basic income would be to give all individuals both autonomy and protection, and to allow them to interact on terms of fairness in whatever society they chose to live and work. This is the same goal as Bauböck's proposals for 'transnational citizenship', which would seem congruent with the NBI approach, and with access to the basic income of the host society of the new entrant only when he or she successfully applies for citizenship, and renounces previous affiliation (and its concomitant NBI). However, during the intervening period, when such entrants might have less (or more) than national citizens, the situation could be unjust by Bauböck's criteria because of the differential between the basic incomes of citizens and non-citizens, even if they had equal rights in all other respects.

From a global perspective, the NBI approach would have another weakness. It would create an incentive for migrants from poor countries, and especially educated and skilled ones, to come to rich ones to settle, and focus pressure and contest around access to citizenship status, rather than (as at present) at borders. This would increase the pull factors leading to 'brain drains' – the ablest individuals in developing countries moving right away from them, rather than working outside them for short- or medium-term stays.

The GBI approach would not be open to any of these objections. It would allow all the world's populations to interact on terms of equality in this limited sense, and be redistributive towards the populations of poor countries. But its level would not be adequate to protect the most vulnerable groups in First World countries, or migrants entering them without other substantial means. In these circumstances, it would be unlikely that the GBI would replace all existing tax and benefit schemes in the richer countries, and hence the other advantages of the basic income approach, in terms of equality, autonomy, security and avoidance of state coercion, would not be achieved.

From an ethical standpoint, the GBI seems the more justifiable approach. If the basic income is to be regarded as part of the 'basic structure of society' – a constitutional right to a substantial form of equality – then it must be derived, in Rawls's contractarian theory, from the original position. And if natural talents are to be regarded as morally arbitrary, how much more should the contingency of being born in a particular country, or the nationality of one's parents, be so regarded? Yet Rawls specifically rules out putting this factor among those to be discounted behind the veil of ignorance: '[T]he original position takes into account only persons contained within . . . society, since we are not considering relations with other societies. That position views society as closed: persons enter only by birth, and exit only by death.'[69]

So Rawls's contract for social justice should, if consistent, prescribe a *global* basis for the basic income (GBI), even though, as a liberal nationalist, he would clearly advocate the NBI approach. Conversely, and equally paradoxically, although Bauböck's recommendation of transnational forms of citizenship sounds like an NBI prescription, the form he would recommend (equal rights to equal rates for all members of any society) would imply something more like a GBI. It seems that the transition towards a basic income transformation might require an NBI approach, but leading towards a GBI goal.

The GBI would make the inhabitants of the poorest countries substantially better off, and would also reduce incentives to migrate to richer countries for all but the top elites, in terms of skills. But few would be able to afford membership of transnational clubs for such collective goods as curative medicine, social care or postgraduate education. This redirects attention back to membership systems for poor people, and especially to those for informal and communal organizations among the poorest groups.

Collectivism and communities of fate

The current model of global governance makes few concessions to states' responsibilities for their least advantaged citizens, or their ways of life. The integration of the world economy has made extinct a whole range of hunter-gatherer lifeworlds, pastoral tribes, peasant communities and proletarian cultures. Global market forces have devastated their eco-systems, their environmental management methods, their social structures and their organizations for solidarity. States have been required to collude in forest felling, connive in new commercial methods, and co-operate with transnational corporate interests in these processes.

However, in the past decade another phenomenon has become apparent – the return to subsistence lifestyles, methods and social systems by those displaced from industrial employments, or locked into impoverished urban ghettos.[70] In First World cities, and throughout the post-communist countries, disadvantaged members of communities of fate have reverted to many of the practices of their rural ancestors. In this sense, they have come to share the fate of Third World populations, whose ways of life do not equip them to compete within the global economy.

These communities share another feature that accentuates their members' vulnerability: that they are prone to organized violence, and give rise to illegal improvizations in the attempt to fill the vacuum left by failures of markets and state systems, and to make some connections with the mainstream economy and mainstream political power. In this section, we sketch the implications of these developments for states as collective actors, trying to address the imperfections of markets, and the social costs of crime, communal violence and the degradation of the cultures through which communities are reproduced. We will argue that there are policies, consistent with the alternative model of membership systems put forward in this chapter, that would allow improvements in the quality of these people's lives.

Imagine a very poor Third World country, in the grip of drought, with a fragile political system, and in heavy debt to foreign banks. Figure 5.1 represents (in a very stark way) the alternatives open to four sections of the population, divided according to their propensities to violence and their tolerance of the risks and discomforts of travelling.

Perhaps as much as 98 per cent of the population might (in the absence of civil war) occupy the travel-averse/non-violent box, living in traditional communities, but reduced to passive options of suffering or illegal economic improv-

	Travel-Averse	*Travel-Tolerant*
Non-violent	Starvation Waiting for food aid Growing drought-resistant drugs	Economic migration Asylum seeking
Violent	Warlordism Mafia activity Crime	International drug dealing International people trafficking Global terrorism

Figure 5.1

izations. Another 1.75 per cent might divide between the travel-averse/violent segments (who coerce and prey upon the first group) and the travel-tolerant/non-violent ones, (who move abroad). Even if only 0.25 per cent become international drug dealers, people traffickers or terrorists, that is enough to pose considerable problems for their own state, and for others, and to call forth the threat of enforcement action by international organizations.

Now imagine the population of a very deprived, excluded urban community in a First World or a post-communist country. The options open to them might be represented (on the same divisions) as shown in Figure 5.2. Again, the bulk of the population would occupy the top left segment, but even small proportions in the bottom two would constitute major disruptions, primarily for local community members, but also for the rest of society, which could bear the costs (stress, fear and paying for the funding of police, prisons and social services) of these activities. Even the reputations of those groups in the wider national community could have very negative consequences for the majority of the local population.

Under the curent model of global governance, policy towards Third World countries by international organizations attempts to block all the options available to the travel-tolerant sections of the population, and increase the

	Travel-Averse	*Travel-Tolerant*
Non-violent	Benefit claims Informal economic activity Drug use	Seeking work further afield Seeking accommodation outside the community
Violent	Petty crime Local gang activity Minor drug dealing	Mobile crime Mafia activity Major drug dealing

Figure 5.2

opportunities for subsistence and (especially) commercial production open to all. In First World and post-communist countries, governments are encouraged to try to activate and motivate those in all the other three boxes to become mobile job-seekers, willing to work, and if necessary to move, outside the community. These policies have been generally unsuccessful, in all types of societies, as the statistics on poverty, inequality, violence and lawlessness testify.

Another whole orientation to the same set of issues is consistent with the alternative regimes in our model. If members of all societies had basic incomes (or in developing countries social dividends, perhaps in the form of land), this could allow policy to focus instead on improving the subsistence capabilities of all such communities, and their overall quality of life. Instead of attempting to extend commercial methods and principles into these marginal districts, and transform local solidarities into cultures of mobile, competitive individualism, these initiatives could aim to resolve local conflicts, and channel activity to common advantage.

This redirects attention towards public services and the collective infrastructure, reviving some of the neglected principles of socialism. As we showed in chapters 1 and 4, the new model of governance treats public services as providing specific professional or nurturing provision for certain needs that individuals have at certain periods in their lives, and not as opportunities for participation in shared activities that create and sustain common interests. Education and health care may be funded by the state, but they are provided by whatever kind of organization, from whatever country, can give 'best value' to individual taxpayers and recipients. The public infrastructure, too, is seen as a set of facilities designed to enable commercial activity, rather than one to sustain convivial shared lifestyles and communal cultures. If subsistence production, infrastructural quality and social relations once more became targets for policy, the *collective* significance of these services would again be paramount. They would be successful in so far as they sustained co-operation in meeting common needs, not merely in terms of individual utility. This applies whether such services are supplied through the state or through non-government organizations.

An example set out in more detail elsewhere[71] is a village project in northern Hungary, in a rural area, before 1989 a region for steel making and mining. With support from a national NGO, a local association acquired all the land in the village and divided it between subsistence plots for each family and collective production for markets. The association comprised Roma and white Hungarian members (who had lacked common networks after they lost their industrial employment), and constituted the main (almost only) economic activity of the community. This form of primitive communism is an ironic return to first principles, in an area that went straight from feudal agriculture to state socialist industry, and then to market failure under capitalism. It illustrated the possibilities of co-operative collective action, and for local government or NGO support to assist in its emergence.

Among international organizations, the World Bank's policies are closest to our preferred model,[72] at least in relation to developing countries. There are limitations in any approach that concentrates on the quality of life of impoverished communities, without improving members' access to the resources that give others advantages, or addressing the lacks that lead to their exclusion. These are not alternatives to education and the other assets that allow mobility and widen the range of available strategies; but they are better than measures that deny basic rights and liberties, that focus solely on suppressing unorthodox improvizations, or that pay disrespect to communal ways of life and cultures of solidarity.

Conclusions

This chapter has aimed at identifying and proposing long-term solutions to the most difficult ethical and policy issues of migration, mobility and membership for the twenty-first century. It has deliberately overlooked short-to medium-term issues of immediate relevance for global inequality and injustice, such as debt crises in developing countries, the rigged terms of trade between these and First World states,[73] and the initial impact of forthcoming GATS measures. It has largely accepted that the integration of the world economy will continue, and that this puts certain constraints on states, but also provides them with certain new opportunities.

Since the start of the new century, immigration has been recognized as part of a solution to many issues in the political economy of First World states, as well as a problem for them. The recruitment of new cohorts of both skilled and unskilled workers promises new dynamism in labour markets, better demographic balances and an injection of innovatory enterprises in small business sectors. Global nomadism is a new way of life, that will open up new possibilities both for nomads and for sedentary populations.

We have argued that migrants who flee the disruptions of home polities and economies are vulnerable to oppression and exploitation, but so are the least mobile members of disadvantaged communities. All such agents need the protection of basic resources for survival in their dealings with corporate and state organizations, and their transactions with more advantaged, better-connected individuals.

Free movement across borders demands a balancing set of rights of primary membership and institutions for including all such members on terms of equal autonomy. If public infrastructures and services can no longer create common interests in the common good of political communities, then the combination of basic incomes for all and collective support for local systems of solidarity must gradually allow new collectivisms to be generated from the grassroots.

Those who most need basic income security among the world's population are citizens of states least fiscally competent to provide it. Neither trade nor aid under the new model of global governance is likely to change this situation. We have not discussed the mechanics of a 'Tobin tax', or the details of a global constitutional order, to enforce collective agreements and integrate decision making under terms that insist on democratic governance and social justice for all populations.[74] Such a re-orientation of the accountability and purposes of an international authority requires a separate analysis, beyond the scope of this short book.

The present global situation is both worse than the one that preceded it, and better. It is worse because, under 'turbo-capitalism' and the transformation of infrastructures, inequalities are growing faster, and injustices against the most vulnerable are increasing. It is better because migration restrictions are being loosened, and the reach of human rights concerns widened. Although globalization makes more people vulnerable, it also forces states and international organizations to take a broader view of issues of equality and justice. Governments cannot turn a blind eye to the plight of those beyond their borders, partly because they are quite likely to present themselves at those borders, applying for admission; or to enter without permission, and establish themselves within their societies.

In the postwar era, welfare state regimes provided versions of equality and justice between citizens, but they obscured issues of global inequality and injustice. Losers from globalization are worse off than they were before the integration of the world economy, and demand new rights, both to migrate, and to have security where they settle. Freedoms of choice over where to live and work are fundamental human rights, but so are the protection of individual vulnerabilities and of common ways of life. Unless states and international organizations develop ways of resolving conflicts of interest between migrants and sedentary people, nationalist and racist agendas, not equality and justice, will be the main themes of the twenty-first century, as they were for the first half of the last one.

Notes

Chapter 1   Introduction: Issues and Perspectives

1   M. Weiner, 'Ethics, National Sovereignty and the Control of Immigration', *International Migration Review*, 30(1), 2000, pp. 67–93, at p. 67.

2   For instance, M. Connelly and P. Kennedy, 'Must it be the Rest against the West?', *Atlantic Monthly*, December, 1994, pp. 61–9. See also J. Rawls, *The Law of Peoples*, Cambridge, MA: Harvard University Press, 1999, p. 39, and p. 125 below.

3   T. Straubhaar, *Why Do We Need a General Agreement on Movements of People (GAMP)?*, HWWA Discussion Paper 94, Hamburg: Hamburg Institute of International Economics; J. Bhagwati, *A Stream of Windows: Unsettling Reflections on Trade, Immigration and Democracy*, Cambridge, MA: MIT Press, 1998.

4   W.E. Oates, 'An Essay on Fiscal Federalism', *Journal of Economic Literature*, 27, 1999, pp. 1120–49.

5   A. Casella and B. Frey, 'Federalism and Clubs: Towards an Economic Theory of Overlapping Political Jurisdictions', *European Economic Review*, 36(2/3), 1992, pp. 639–46.

6   For liberal and socialist critiques, see Z. Bauman, *Globalization: The Human Consequences*, Cambridge: Polity, 1998, and A. Callinicos, *Equality*, Cambridge: Polity, 2000. For an ethical evaluation of migration policies, see P. Cole, *Philosophies of Exclusion: Liberal Political Theory and Immigration*, Edinburgh: Edinburgh University Press, 2000.

7   J.E. Stiglitz, *Globalization and Its Discontents*, London: Allen Lane, 2002, ch. 9.

8   For example, Oxfam, 'Rigged Rules and Double Standards: Trade, Globalization and the Fight Against Poverty', press release, 24 April 2002.

9   A. Sivanandan, 'Refugees from Globalism', *CARF*, 57(8/9), 2000, pp. 10–12.

10 F. Williams, *Social Policy: A Critical Introduction*, Cambridge: Polity, 1989.

11 R. Boyer, 'The Political in the Era of Globalization and Finance: Focus on some *Régulation* School Research', *International Journal of Urban and Regional Research*, 24, 2000, pp. 275–322, at p. 280.

12 A.D. Chandler, 'What is a Firm? A Historical Perspective', *European Economic Review*, 36(2/3), 1992, pp. 483–92.

13 G. Esping-Andersen, *The Three Worlds of Welfare Capitalism*, Cambridge: Polity, 1990.

14 Boyer, 'The Political in the Era of Globalization and Finance', p. 294.

15 Ibid., pp. 290–2.

16 Ibid., p. 295.

17 E. Luttwak, *Turbo-capitalism: Winners and Losers in the Global Economy*, New York: Weidenfeld and Nicolson, 1999; A. Portes, 'Globalization from Below: The Rise of Transnational Communities', WPTC 98–01, ESRC Transnational Communities Programme, Oxford: Oxford University, 1998; M.P. Smith and L.E. Guarnizo (eds), *Transnationalism from Below*, New Brunswick, NJ: Transaction Books, 1998.

18 Stiglitz, *Globalization and Its Discontents*, ch. 3.

19 Chandler, 'What is a Firm?', p. 487.

20 A.C. Pigou, *The Economics of Welfare*, London: Macmillan, 1920.

21 A. Cornes and T. Sandler, *The Theory of Externalities, Public Goods and Club Goods*, Cambridge: Cambridge University Press, 1986, ch. 11.

22 J.M. Buchanan, 'An Economic Theory of Clubs', *Economica*, 32, 1965, pp. 1–14.

23 Casella and Frey, 'Federalism and Clubs'.

24 Cornes and Sandler, *The Theory of Externalities, Public Goods and Club Goods*, pp. 194–5.

25 D. Whitfield, *Public Services or Corporate Welfare?*, London: Pluto Press, 2001, p. 114.

26 R. Hatcher, *The Business of Education: How Business Agendas Drive Labour Policies for Schools*, Stafford: Socialist Educational Association, 2001; D. Price, A.M. Pollock and J. Shaoul, 'How the World Trade Organization is Shaping Domestic Policies in Health Care', *The Lancet*, 354(27), pp. 1889–92, especially p. 1891. World Development Movement, *Out of Service: The Development Dangers of The General Agreement on Trade in Services*, London: World Development Movement, 2002.

27 Gordon Brown, UK Chancellor of the Exchequer, speech at Leeds, reported in the *Guardian*, 29 March 2002.

28 R. Hatcher, 'Getting Down to Business: Schooling in the Globalised Economy', *Education and Social Justice*, 3(2), 2001, pp. 45–59, at p. 51.

29 Ibid.

30 World Trade Organization, *Annual Report, 2001*, Geneva: World Trade Organization, 2001, p. 2.

31 Quoted in Hugo Young, 'A New Imperialism Cooked up over a Texan Barbecue', *Guardian*, 2 April 2002.

32 R. Cooper, *Reordering the World*, London: Foreign Policy Centre, 2002.

33 S. Krasner, *Sovereignty: Organized Hypocrisy*, Princeton, NJ: Princeton University Press, 1999.

34 D. Held, A. McGrew, D. Goldblatt and J. Perraton, *Global Transformations: Politics, Economics and Culture*, Cambridge: Polity, 1999, pp. 55, 69.

35 See, for instance, A. Gutmann, *Liberal Equality*, Cambridge: Cambridge University Press, 1980, p. 18; W. Kymlicka, *Contemporary Political Philosophy: An Introduction*, Oxford: Clarendon Press, 1990, pp. 36–7; Cole, *Philosophies of Exclusion*, pp. 3–4.

36 W.I. Jennings, *The Approach to Self-government*, Cambridge: Cambridge University Press, 1956, p. 56.

37   R. Bauböck, *Transnational Citizenship: Membership and Rights in International Migration*, Aldershot: Edward Elgar, 1994, p. 178.

38   Cole, *Philosophies of Social Exclusion*, p. 161.

39   A. Geddes, *Immigration and European Integration: Towards Fortress Europe*, Manchester: Manchester University Press, 2000; A. Lavenex, *The Europeanisation of Refugee Policies: Between Human Rights and Internal Security*, Aldershot: Ashgate, 2001.

40   European Commission, *Communication from the Commission to the Council and the European Parliament on a Concerted Strategy for Immigration and Asylum* (Mr Vitorino and Mrs Diamantopoulos), COM (2000) 757 final, Brussels: European Commission, 2000.

41   European Commission, *Communication on a Common Policy on Illegal Immigration*, COM (2001) 672 final, Brussels: European Commission, 2001.

42   European Commission, Liaison Officers: Common Use of Liaison Officers in the EU Member States, note from the Presidency to Police Co-operation Working Party, 5406/1 Enfopol, 17 January, Brussels: European Commission, 2001.

43   Weiner, 'Ethics, National Sovereignty and the Control of Immigration'; for critical analyses of this perspective, see B. Barry and R.E. Goodin (eds), *Free Movement: Ethical Issues in the Transnational Migration of People and Money*, University Park, PA: Pennsylvania State University Press, 1992, and W.F. Schwartz (ed.), *Justice in Immigration*, Cambridge: Cambridge University Press, 1995.

44   World Bank, *World Development Report 2000/2001: Attacking Poverty*, Washington, DC: World Bank/Oxford University Press, 2001.

45   Bauböck, *Transnational Citizenship*.

46   R. Nozick, *Anarchy, State and Utopia*, Oxford: Blackwell, 1974.

47   A.O. Sykes, 'The Welfare Economics of Immigration Law: A Theoretical Survey with an Analysis of US Policy', in Schwartz (ed.), *Justice in Immigration*, pp. 158–200.

48 R.P. Inman and D.L. Rubinfeld, 'The Political Economy of Federalism', in D.C. Mueller (ed.), *Perspectives on Public Choice: A Handbook*, Cambridge: Cambridge University Press, 1997, pp. 73–105.

49 C. Tiebout, 'A Pure Theory of Local Expenditures', *Journal of Political Economy*, 64, 1956, pp. 416–24.

50 Bauman, *Globalization*.

51 A.O. Hirschman, *Exit, Voice and Loyalty: Responses to Decline in Firms, Organizations and States*, Cambridge, MA: Harvard University Press, 1970.

52 Ibid., pp. 69–71.

53 For such instances, see B. Jordan and F. Düvell, *Irregular Migration: The Dilemmas of Transnational Mobility*, Cheltenham: Edward Elgar, 2002, ch. 9.

54 Ibid., chs 4 and 5.

55 M. Dummett, *Immigration and Refugees*, London: Routledge, 2001.

56 J. Salt and J. Clarke, 'Foreign Labour in the UK: Patterns and Trends', *Labour Market Trends*, October 2001, pp. 1173–83.

57 Jordan and Düvell, *Irregular Migration*, chs 4 and 5.

58 BBC Radio 4, *The World at One*, 27 March 2002.

Chapter 2   The New Model of Global Governance

1 J.E. Stiglitz, *Globalization and Its Discontents*, London: Allen Lane, 2002.

2 P. van Parijs, 'Commentary: Citizenship, Exploitation, Unequal Exchange and the Breakdown of Popular Sovereignty', in B. Barry and R.E. Goodin (eds), *Free Movement: Ethical Issues in the Transnational Migration of People and Money*, University Park, PA: Pennsylvania University Press, 1992, pp. 155–66.

3 A. Casella and B. Frey, 'Federalism and Clubs: Towards an Economic Theory of Overlapping Political Jurisdictions', *European Economic Review*, 36(2/3), 1992, pp. 639–46.

4 C. Tiebout, 'A Pure Theory of Local Expenditures', *Journal of Political Economy*, 64, 1956, pp. 416–24.

5 A.O. Hirschman, *Exit, Voice and Loyalty: Responses to Decline in Firms, Organizations and States*, Cambridge, MA: Harvard University Press, 1970.

6 B. Jordan and F. Düvell, *Irregular Migration: The Dilemmas of Transnational Mobility*, Cheltenham: Edward Elgar, 2002, chs 2 and 9.

7 Stiglitz, *Globalization and Its Discontents*, ch. 1.

8 Ibid., pp. 64–5, 98–104.

9 Ibid., pp. 6–7, 61–2, 172–6.

10 D. Begg, S. Fischer and R. Dornbusch, *Economics* (3rd edn), Maidenhead: McGraw-Hill, 1991, p. 187.

11 M. Olson, *The Logic of Collective Action: Public Goods and the Theory of Groups*, Cambridge, MA: Harvard University Press, 1965.

12 B. Jordan, *A Theory of Poverty and Social Exclusion*, Cambridge: Polity, 1996, pp. 58–60.

13 The distinction between institutions and organizations is made by D.C. North, *Institutions, Institutional Change and Economic Performance*, Cambridge: Cambridge University Press, 1990, p. 4.

14 Stiglitz, *Globalization and Its Discontents*, chs 5 and 7.

15 Ibid., p. 143.

16 For instance, A. Aslund and A. Warner, 'The EU Enlargement: The Consequences for the CIS Countries', paper presented at a conference, 'Beyond Transition', CASE Foundation, Warsaw, Poland, 12–13 April 2002.

17 European Bank for Reconstruction and Development (EBRD), *Transition Report, 2001*, London: EBRD, 2001, p. 59.

18 World Bank, *World Development Indicators*, Washington, DC: World Bank, 2000.

19 Ibid.

20 R. Layard, 'How to Make National Labour Markets More Flexible', paper prepared for a conference, 'Beyond Transition'.

21 C.J. Smith, 'The Transformative Impact of Capital and

Labour Mobility on the Chinese City', *Urban Geography*, 21(8), 2000, pp. 670–700.

22 A. Findlay, H. Jones and G.M. Davidson, 'Migration Transitions or Migration Transformation in the Asian Dragon Economies?', *International Journal of Urban and Regional Research*, 22(4), 1998, pp. 643–64.

23 Stiglitz, *Globalization and Its Discontents*, pp. 182–6.

24 Ibid., pp. 64–5.

25 Ibid., pp. 185–7.

26 Ibid., p. 186.

27 A. Berg, E. Borensztein and P. Mauro, 'An Evaluation of Monetary Regime Options for Latin America', paper prepared for a conference, 'Beyond Transition'.

28 P. Mitra and N. Stern (World Bank), 'Tax Reform in Transition', paper prepared for a conference 'Beyond Transition', p. 1.

29 S. Johnson, P. Boone, A. Breach and E. Friedman, 'Corporate Governance in the Asian Financial Crisis', *Journal of Financial Economics*, 58, 2000, pp. 141–86.

30 P. Mihályi, 'Foreign Direct Investment in Hungary: The Post-communist Privatization Story Re-considered', *Acta Oeconomica*, 51(1), 2001, pp. 107–29.

31 Stiglitz, *Globalization and Its Discontents*, p. 154.

32 World Bank, *World Development Report 2000/2001: Attacking Poverty*, Washington, DC: World Bank/Oxford University Press, 2001, p. 3.

33 Ibid., pp. 6–7.

34 Ibid., pp. 34–41.

35 Ibid., chs 5 and 6.

36 Ibid., p. 85.

37 Ibid., pp. 86–93, 110–11.

38 P. Dasgupta and I. Serageldin (eds), *Social Capital: A Multifaceted Perspective*, Washington, DC: World Bank, 2000.

39 World Bank, *World Development Report, 2000/2001*, p. 10.

40 Ibid., p. 131.

41 Ibid., p. 10.

42 Ibid., ch. 4.

43   Ibid., p. 80.

44   H. Spruyt, *The Sovereign State and Its Competitors: An Analysis of Systems Change*, Princeton, NJ: Princeton University Press, 1994, ch. 4.

45   Ibid., chs 6 and 7.

46   R.P. Inman and D.L. Rubinfeld, 'The Political Economy of Federalism', in D.C. Mueller (ed.), *Perspectives on Public Choice: A Handbook*, Cambridge: Cambridge University Press, 1997, pp. 73–105.

47   G. Brennan and J. Buchanan, *The Power to Tax: Analytical Foundations of a Fiscal Constitution*, Cambridge: Cambridge University Press, 1980.

48   For instance, between Selden, Filmer, Hobbes, Pufendorf and Locke. See B. Jordan, *The State: Authority and Autonomy*, Oxford: Blackwell, 1985, ch. 2.

49   For instance, between Rousseau, Montesquieu, Hume, Jefferson and Madison. See ibid., ch. 4.

50   For instance Bentham, J.S. Mill and Dicey. See ibid., chs 5 and 6.

51   W.A. Niskanen, 'Bureaucrats and Politicians', *Journal of Law and Economics*, 18, 1975, pp. 617–43.

52   W.E. Oates, 'Searching for Leviathan: An Empirical Study', *American Economic Review*, 75, 1985, pp. 748–57; Brennan and Buchanan, *The Power to Tax*.

53   W.E. Oates, 'An Essay on Fiscal Federalism', *Journal of Economic Literature*, 27, 1999, pp. 1120–49, at p. 1122.

54   W.E. Oates, *Fiscal Federalism*, New York: Harcourt Brace Jovanovich, 1972.

55   Oates, 'An Essay on Fiscal Federalism', p. 1122.

56   R. Bauböck, *Transnational Citizenship: Membership and Rights in International Migration*, Aldershot: Edward Elgar, 1994, p. 14; Inman and Rubinfeld, 'The Political Economy of Federalism', pp. 73–4.

57   R.H. Coase, 'The Problem of Social Cost', *Journal of Law and Economics*, 3, 1960, pp. 1–44.

58   Inman and Rubinfeld, 'The Political Economy of Federalism', pp. 75–6.

59   Ibid.

60 Oates, 'An Essay in Fiscal Federalism', p. 1122.
61 C. Tiebout, 'A Pure Theory of Local Expenditures'. See also A. Breton, *Competitive Governments: An Economic Theory of Politics and Public Finance*, Cambridge: Cambridge University Press, 1998.
62 Inman and Rubinfeld, 'The Political Economy of Federalism', p. 81.
63 J. Cullis and P. Jones, *Public Finance and Public Choice: Analytical Perspectives*, London: McGraw Hill, 1994, pp. 300–2.
64 Ibid.
65 R.I. McKinnon, 'Market-Preserving Fiscal Federalism in the American Monetary Union', in M. Blejer and T. Ter-Minassian (eds), *Macroeconomic Dimension of Public Finance: Essays in Honor of Vito Tanzi*, London: Routledge, 1997, pp. 73–93; B.R. Weingast, 'The Economic Role of Political Institutions: Market-Preserving Federalism and Economic Development', *Journal of Law and Economic Organization*, 11, 1995, pp. 1–31.
66 Oates, 'An Essay of Fiscal Federalism', pp. 1139, 1143.
67 W.E. Oates and R.M. Schwab, 'The Impact of Urban Land Taxes: The Pittsburgh Experience', *National Tax Journal*, 50, 1997, pp. 1–21.
68 Inman and Rubinfeld, 'The Political Economy of Federalism', p. 105.
69 Oates, 'An Essay on Fiscal Federalism', p. 1131; B. Ackerman, S. Rose-Ackerman, J.W. Sawyer and D.W. Henderson, *The Uncertain Search for Environmental Quality*, New York: Free Press, 1974; W.E. Oates and R.M. Schwab, 'The Theory of Regulatory Federalism: The Case of Environmental Management', in W.E. Oates (ed.), *The Political Economy of Fiscal Federalism*, Lexington, MA: Heath-Lexington, pp. 275–355.
70 J.K. Brueckner, 'Welfare Reform and the Race to the Bottom: Theory and Evidence', *Southern Economic Journal*, 66(3), 2000, pp. 505–25.
71 Oates, 'An Essay on Fiscal Federalism', p. 1127.
72 International Development Association, *Poverty Reduction*

Strategy Papers and IDA 13, Washington, DC: International Development Association, May 2001, p. 13.

73 Ibid.

74 Ibid., p. 11.

75 World Bank, *World Development Report 2000/2001: Attacking Poverty*, box 3.3, p. 51.

76 Ibid.

77 Ibid., pp. 53–5.

78 Ibid., box 3.6, p. 55.

79 Ibid., box 3.5, p. 54.

80 A. Cornes and T. Sandler, *The Theory of Externalities, Public Goods, and Club Goods*, Cambridge: Cambridge University Press, 1986, ch. 11.

81 E. Luttwak, *Turbo-capitalism: Winners and Losers in the Global Economy*, New York: Weidenfeld and Nicolson, 1999.

Chapter 3 The Political Economy of Migration

1 M. Weiner, *The Global Migration Crisis: Challenge to States and to Human Rights*, New York: HarperCollins, 1995, p. 22.

2 F. Thistlethwaite, 'Migration, Ethnicity and the Rise of an Atlantic Economy', in R.J. Vecoli and S.M. Sinke (eds), *A Century of European Migrations, 1830–1930*, Urbana, IL: University of Illinois Press, 1991, pp. 17–57.

3 P. Cole, *Philosophies of Exclusion: Liberal Political Theory and Immigration*, Edinburgh: Edinburgh University Press, 2000, chs 2 and 3.

4 A. Zolberg, 'Changing Sovereignty Games and International Migration', *Global Legal Studies Journal*, 2(1), 1994, pp. 153–77.

5 P.A. Fischer, E. Holm, G. Malmberg and T. Straubhaar, *Why Do People Stay? Insider Advantages and Immobility*, HWW Discussion Paper 112, Hamburg: Institute of International Economics, 2000.

6 A. Portes and J. Böröcz, 'Contemporary Immigration: The-

oretical Perspectives on Its Determination and Modes of Implementation', *International Migration Review*, 23(3), 1989, pp. 606–30.

7 S. Sassen, *The Mobility of Labor and Capital: A Study in International Investment and Labor Flow*, Cambridge: Cambridge University Press, 1988.

8 S. Sassen, *The Global City: New York, London, Tokyo*, Princeton, NJ: Princeton University Press, 1991.

9 A. Böcker, 'Chain Migration over Legally Closed Borders: Settled Migrants as Bridgeheads and Gatekeepers', *Netherlands Journal of Sociology*, 30(2), 1994, pp. 87–106.

10 S. Vertovec and R. Cohen, *Migration, Diasporas and Transnationalism*, Cheltenham: Edward Elgar, 1999.

11 R.L. Bach and L.A. Schraml, 'Migration, Crisis and Theoretical Conflict', *International Migration Review*, 16(2), 1982, pp. 320–41.

12 A. Portes, 'Globalization from Below: The Rise of Transnational Communities', ESRC Transnational Communities Programme, WPCT 98–01, ESRC Transnational Communities Programme, Oxford: Oxford University, 1998.

13 F. Pieke, 'Fujianese Migration to the UK: Implications for Policy Making', paper presented at a seminar on 'Low-Skilled Migration', Institute for Public Policy Research, London, 15 March 2002.

14 A. Sivanandan, 'Refugees from Globalism', *CARF*, 57(8/9), 2000, pp. 10–12.

15 Weiner, *The Global Migration Crisis*; and 'Ethics, National Sovereignty and the Control of Immigration', *International Migration Review*, 30(1), 2000, pp. 67–93.

16 UNHCR Population Data Unit, *1993, UNHCR Population Statistics*, Geneva: UNHCR, 1994.

17 UNHCR Population Data Unit, *2001 UNHCR Population Statistics (Provisional)*, Geneva: UNHCR, 15 May 2002.

18 Fischer et al., *Why Do People Stay?* In 1998, Mills gave the figure of 80 to 100 million, and argued that the proportion (2 per cent of the world's population) had not changed since the 1970s, though the absolute numbers have. How-

ever, if internal migration, especially between rural and urban areas in large countries such as India, China, Nigeria, Brazil, Indonesia and Mexico, is taken into account, the figure of 500 million may be more accurate. See K. Mills, *Human Rights in the Emerging Global Order: A New Sovereignty?*, New York: St Martin's Press, 1998, p. 97.

19   UNHCR Population Data Unit, *2001 UNHCR Population Statistics (Provisional)*, Geneva: UNHCR, 2 May 2002. However, the number of asylum seekers in North America (440,000) and Europe (320,000) was higher than those elsewhere, in a world total of 926,000 (ibid.)

20   Ibid.

21   P. Kennedy, *Preparing for the Twenty-First Century*, New York: Random House, 1993, pp. 44–5.

22   Thistlethwaite, 'Migration, Ethnicity and the Rise of an Atlantic Economy'.

23   Weiner, *The Global Migration Crisis*, p. 26.

24   Ibid.

25   Ibid., table 18, p. 202.

26   Ibid., table 19, p. 203.

27   Ibid.

28   Fischer et al., *Why Do People Stay?*; Mills, *Human Rights in the Emerging Global Order*.

29   Weiner, *The Global Migration Crisis*, table 1, p. 6.

30   Ibid., table 2, p. 7.

31   A. Entorf, *Rational Migration Policy Should Tolerate Non-Zero Illegal Migration Flows: Lessons for Modelling the Market for Illegal Migration*, Discussion Paper 1999, Bonn: IZA, 2000, p. 1.

32   Ibid., p. 1; 33 million, summing figures from more than forty states (F. Düvell, 'Migration, Krise und die Modernisierung des Migrationsregimes', in *Materialen gegen imperialistische Fluchtlingspolitik*, Berlin: Assoziation A, 2002, pp. 45–168. An IOM source gives the figure of 15 to 30 million (International Office of Migration, *Assisted Return Service*, www.iom/new.htm, undated). The latest figures are reckoned to be 5 million for the USA and the same for Europe.

33 D. de Bruycker, *Regularisations of Illegal Immigrants in the European Union*, Brussels: Bruylant, 2000.

34 F. Düvell and B. Jordan, 'Immigration, Asylum and Welfare: The European Context', *Critical Social Policy*, 22(3), 2002, pp. 498–517.

35 European Commission, *Communication from the Commission to the Council and the European Parliament on a Concerted Strategy for Immigration and Asylum* (Mr Vitorino and Mrs Diamantopoulos), COM (2000) 757 final, Brussels: European Commission, 2000; Home Office, *Secure Borders, Safe Haven: Integration with Diversity in Modern Britain* (White Paper), London: Stationery Office, 2002, ch. 3.

36 European Commission, *Communication from the Commission to the Council and the European Parliament on a Common Policy on Illegal Immigration*, COM (2001) 672 final, Brussels: European Commission, 2001; Home Office, *Secure Borders, Safe Haven*, ch. 5.

37 E. Luttwak, *Turbo-capitalism: Winners and Losers in the Global Economy*, New York: Weidenfeld and Nicolson, 1999; A. Callinicos, *Equality*, Cambridge: Polity, 2000.

38 Portes and Böröcz, 'Contemporary Immigration'.

39 J. Salt, 'A Comparative Overview of International Trends and Types, 1950–80', *International Migration Review*, 23, 1989, pp. 431–56.

40 H. Jones and A. Findlay, 'Regional Economic Integration and the Emergence of the East Asian International Migration System', *Geoforum*, 29(4), 1998, pp. 401–27.

41 Ibid.

42 E.F. Pang, 'Labour Migration in the Newly Industrialising Economies of South Korea, Hong Kong and Singapore, *International Migration*, 31, 1993, pp. 300–13.

43 A. Findlay, H. Jones and G. Davidson, 'Migration Transition or Migration Transformation in the Asian Dragon Economies?', *International Journal of Urban and Regional Research*, 22(4), 1998, pp. 643–64.

44 Jones and Findlay, 'Regional Economic Integration'.

45 Ibid.

46 Ibid.
47 Findlay et al., 'Migration Transition or Migration Trans-
    formation in the Asian Dragon Economies?'
48 Ibid.; S. Castles, 'Asia-Pacific Migration and Emerging
    Civil Societies', *Asian Migrant*, 10(2), 1997, pp. 41–8.
49 A. Portes and S. Sassen-Koob, 'Making it Underground:
    Comparative Material on the Informal Sector in Western
    Market Economies', *American Journal of Sociology*, 1987,
    pp. 30–61.
50 L.G. Basch, N. Glick Schiller and C. Blanc-Szanton,
    *Nations Unbound: Transnational Projects, Post-colonial Predic-
    aments, and De-territorialized Nation States*, Langhome, PA:
    Gordon and Breach, 1994.
51 A. Portes, 'Globalization from Below'.
52 A. Portes and L.E. Guarnizo, 'Tropical Capitalists: US-
    bound Immigration and Small Enterprise Development in
    the Dominican Republic', in S. Diaz-Briquets and S. Wein-
    traub (eds), *Migration Remittances and Business Development,
    Mexico and the Caribbean Basin Countries*, Boulder, CO:
    Westview Press, 1990, pp. 101–31.
53 Pieke, 'Fujianese Migration'.
54 B. Jordan and F. Düvell, *Irregular Migration: The Dilemmas
    of Transnational Mobility*, Cheltenham: Edward Elgar,
    2002, chs 4 and 5.
55 J. Rath, 'The Informal Economy as a Bastard Sphere of
    Social Integration: The Case of Amsterdam', in E. Eichen-
    hofer (ed.), *Migration und Illegalität*, Osnabrück: Universi-
    tätsverlag Rasch, 1999, pp. 117–36.
56 Düvell and Jordan, *Irregular Migration*, ch. 5.
57 Ibid.
58 Ibid., ch. 7.
59 T. Faist, *Transnationalization in International Migration:
    Implications for the Study of Citizenship and Culture*, WPTC-
    99–08, ESRC Transnational Communities Programme,
    Oxford: Oxford University; L. Pries, 'The Approach of
    Transnational Social Spaces: Responding to New Con-
    figurations of the Social and the Spatial', in his *New
    Transnational Social Spaces: International Migration and*

Transnational Companies in the Early Twenty-First Century, London: Routledge, 2000.

60 Faist, *Transnationalization*, p. 4.

61 Ibid., p. 8.

62 B. Anderson, 'Different Roots in Common Ground: Transnationalism and Migrant Domestic Workers in London', *Journal of Ethnic and Migration Studies*, 27(4), 2001, pp. 673–83.

63 L.E. Guarnizo and M.P. Smith, 'The Locations of Transnationalism', in M.P. Smith and L.E. Guarnizo (eds), *Transnationalism from Below*, New Brunswick, NJ: Transaction Books, 1998, pp. 64–100.

64 B. Jordan and D. Vogel, 'Which Policies Influence Migration Decisions? A Comparative Analysis of Qualitative Interviews with Undocumented Brazilian Immigrants in London and Berlin as a Contribution to Economic Reasoning', ZeS Arbeitspapier 14/97, Bremen: University of Bremen, Centre for Social Policy Research, 1997.

65 Ibid., pp. 17–19.

66 A. Triandafyllidou and M. Veikou, 'Immigration Control Policy in Italy: Organizational Culture, Identity Processes and Labour Market Control', paper presented at a seminar on Immigration Control, Exeter University, 3–5 March 2001.

67 Jordan and Düvell, *Irregular Migration*, pp. 178–81.

68 Jordan and Vogel, 'Which Policies Influence Migration Decisions?', pp. 12–13.

69 Ibid., p. 19.

70 A. Kosic and A. Triandafyllidou, 'Making Sense of Italy as a Host Country: A Qualitative Analysis of Immigrant Discourse', and I. Psimmenos and K. Kassimati, 'Albanian and Polish Workers' Life-Stories: Migration Paths, Tactics and Identities in Greece', papers presented at a seminar on 'Migrants' Strategies', European University Institute, Florence, 22–23 February 2002.

71 Jordan and Düvell, *Irregular Migration*, pp. 102, 133.

72 J.N. Bhagwati and J.D. Wilson, *Income Taxation and International Mobility*, Cambridge, MA: MIT Press, 1989.

73   Jordan and Düvell, *Irregular Migration*, ch. 5.

74   Home Office, *Secure Borders, Safe Haven*, ch. 3.

75   O. Blanchard, 'Labour Market Flexibility and Labour Market Institutions', paper presented at a conference, 'Beyond Transition', CASE Foundation, Warsaw, 12–13 April 2002.

76   Home Office, *Fairer, Faster and Firmer: A Modern Approach to Immigration and Asylum*, Cm 4018, London: Stationery Office, 1998, sec. 1.7.

77   F. Düvell and B. Jordan, 'The Immigrants' Perspective: Migration Patterns, Migration Strategies and Identities in the UK', paper presented at a seminar on 'Migrants' Strategies'.

78   J. Salt and J. Clarke, 'Foreign Labour in the United Kingdom: Patterns and Trends', *Labour Market Trends*, October, pp. 473–83.

79   J. Dobson, G. McLaughlan and J. Salt, 'International Migration and the United Kingdom: Recent Patterns and Trends', in Home Office, *Bridging the Information Gaps: A Conference of Research on Asylum and Immigration*, 1 Whitehall Place, London, 21 March 2001, pp. 66–70.

80   Jordan and Düvell, *Irregular Migration*, pp. 230–2.

81   Ibid., pp. 145–6.

82   K. Schlögel, 'Planet der Nomaden', in his *Die Mitte liegt oftwärts: Europa in Übergang*, Munich: Hanser, 2002, pp. 65–133.

Chapter 4   Cosmopolitan Economic Membership

1   R. Dworkin, 'What Is Equality? Part II: Equality of Resources', *Philosophy and Public Affairs*, 10, 1981, pp. 283–345; A. Gutmann, *Liberal Equality*, Cambridge: Cambridge University Press, 1980, pp. 18, 34–7.

2   W. Kymlicka, *Contemporary Political Philosophy: An Introduction*, Oxford: Clarendon Press, 1990, p. 44.

3   P. Cole, *Philosophies of Exclusion: Liberal Political Theory and*

Immigration, Edinburgh: Edinburgh University Press, 2000, p. 2.

4 J. Rawls, *Political Liberalism*, New York: Columbia University Press, 1993, p. 181.

5 Cole, *Philosophies of Exclusion*, pp. 193–5.

6 Ibid., p. 136.

7 Ibid., p. 161.

8 For example, D. Miller, *On Nationality*, Oxford: Clarendon Press, 1995.

9 This is Cole's assessment of Miller, ibid.; see Cole, *Philosophies of Exclusion*, p. 108.

10 Y. Tamir, *Liberal Nationalism*, Princeton, NJ: Princeton University Press, 1993.

11 F.G. Whelan, 'Citizenship and Freedom of Movement: An Open Admissions Policy?', in M. Gibney (ed.), *Open Borders? Closed Societies? The Ethical and Political Issues*, Westport, CT: Greenwood Press, 1988, pp. 8–16.

12 Cole, *Philosophies of Exclusion*, ch. 8.

13 R. Nozick, *Anarchy, State and Utopia*, Oxford: Blackwell, 1974; H. Steiner, 'Libertarianism and the Transnational Migration of People', in B. Barry and R.E. Goodin (eds), *Free Movement: Ethical Issues in the Transnational Migration of People and Money*, University Park, PA: Pennsylvania State University Press, 1992, pp. 87–94.

14 B. Jordan, *A Theory of Poverty and Social Exclusion*, Cambridge: Polity, 1996.

15 F.A. Hayek, *New Studies in Philosophy, Politics and Economics*, London: Routledge and Kegan Paul, 1978, ch. 1.

16 Ibid.

17 J. Rawls, *A Theory of Justice*, Oxford: Oxford University Press, 1971.

18 Cole, *Philosophies of Exclusion*, ch. 9.

19 J. Locke, *Second Treatise of Government* (1698), ed. P. Laslett, Cambridge: Cambridge University Press, 1967, secs 184–5.

20 Ibid., secs 82 and 83.

21 J. Locke, Board of Trade Papers, Journal B., pp. 242–326, quoted in H.R. Fox Bourne, *The Life of John Locke*, Lon-

don: King, 1876, pp. 377–87. See also 'Some Considerations of the Consequences of the Lowering of Interest, and Raising the Value of Money', in *The Works of John Locke in Four Volumes*, Edinburgh: W. Strachan et al., 1777, Vol. II, pp. 10–46.

22   Locke, *Second Treatise*, secs. 183–7; J.S. Mill, 'Some Considerations Concerning Representative Government', in *Utilitarianism, Liberty, Representative Government*, London: Dent, 1912, pp. 197–8. For Kant's views, see E.C. Eze, 'The Color of Reason: The Idea of "Race" in Kant's Anthropology', in E.C. Eze (ed.), *Post-colonial African Philosophy: A Critical Reader*, Oxford: Blackwell, 1997, pp. 99–127, especially p. 115.

23   J.S. Mill, 'Principles of Political Economy, with Some of Their Applications to Social Philosophy' (1848), *Collected Works*, ed. J.M. Robson, London: Routledge and Kegan Paul, 1967, vols 2 and 3, book II, ch. xii, sec. 2.

24   T.H. Marshall, *Citizenship and Social Class*, Cambridge: Cambridge University Press, 1950.

25   H.H. Hoppe, 'Free Immigration or Forced Integration?', *Salisbury Review*, June 1995, pp. 17–20.

26   T. Wragg, 'Wise Words', *Guardian Education*, 6 August 2002.

27   *Guardian*, 22 May 2002.

28   L.M. Mead, *Beyond Entitlement: The Social Obligations of Citizenship*, New York: Free Press.

29   International Development Association, *Poverty Reduction Strategy Papers and IDA 13*, Washington, DC: International Development Association, May 2001, p. 13.

30   Ibid.

31   Heritage Foundation/*Wall Street Journal*, *Index of Economic Freedom*, New York: Heritage Foundation.

32   S. Sassen, *The Mobility of Labor and Capital: A Study in International Investment and Labor Flow*, Cambridge: Cambridge University Press, 1988, ch. 5; S. Sassen, *The Global City: New York, London, Tokyo*, Princeton, NJ: Princeton University Press, 1991.

33   R. Bauböck, *Transnational Citizenship: Membership and*

Rights in International Migration, Aldershot: Edward Elgar, 1994, p. 172.

34 Sassen, *The Global City*; B. Jordan and F. Düvell, *Irregular Migration: The Dilemmas of Transnational Mobility*, Cheltenham: Edward Elgar, 2002, chs 4 and 5.

35 J. Rawls, 'Constitutional Liberty and the Concept of Justice', in C.J. Friedrich and J.W. Chapman (eds), *Justice: Nomos VI*, New York: Atherton, 1963, pp. 117–39.

36 See, for instance, M. Rhodes and Y. Mény, 'Europe's Social Contract Under Stress', in M. Rhodes and Y. Mény (eds), *The Future of European Welfare: A New Social Contract*, Basingstoke: Macmillan, 1998, pp. 1–20; F.W. Scharpf, *The Viability of Advanced Welfare States in the International Economy: Vulnerabilities and Options*, Working Paper 99–9, Cologne: Max Planck Institute for the Study of Societies, 1999.

37 Bauböck, *Transnational Citizenship*, p. 235.

38 J. Habermas, *The Structural Transformation of the Public Sphere*, Cambridge: Polity, 1989.

39 Bauböck, *Transnational Citizenship*, p. 209.

40 Ibid., p. 227.

41 A. Sen, *Inequality Re-examined*, Oxford: Oxford University Press, 1992, pp. 39–40; and 'Rights and Capabilities', in his *Resources, Values and Development*, Oxford: Blackwell, 1984, pp. 307–24.

42 A. Sen, 'Equality of What?', in his *Choice, Welfare and Measurement*, Oxford: Oxford University Press, 1982, pp. 353–69.

43 See, for instance, H. Arendt, *Men in Dark Times*, San Diego, CA: Harvest Books, 1970.

44 Bauböck, *Transnational Citizenship*, p. 299.

45 Ibid., p. 230.

46 C. Tiebout, 'A Pure Theory of Local Expenditures', *Journal of Political Economy*, 64, 1956, pp. 416–24; W.E. Oates, *Fiscal Federalism*, New York: Harcourt Brace Jovanovich, 1972.

47 J.M. Buchanan, 'An Economic Theory of Clubs', *Economica*, 32, 1965, pp. 1–14; J. Cullis and P. Jones, *Public*

Finance and Public Choice: Analytical Perspectives, London: McGraw-Hill, 1994, p. 300.

48 Cullis and Jones, *Public Finance and Public Choice*, p. 297.

49 Ibid., p. 300.

50 F. Foldvary, *Public Goods and Private Communities: The Market Provision of Social Services*, Aldershot: Edward Elgar, 1994.

51 Bauböck, *Transnational Citizenship*, p. 274.

52 *Guardian*, 18 March 2002.

53 Jordan, *A Theory of Poverty and Social Exclusion*, ch. 5.

54 B. Jordan, M. Redley and S. James, *Putting the Family First: Identities, Decisions, Citizenship*, London: UCL Press, 1994.

55 E.O. Erikson and J. Weigård, 'The End of Citizenship?', in C. McKinnon and I. Hampsher-Monk (eds), *The Demands of Citizenship*, London: Continuum, 2000, pp. 13–34; C. Crouch, K. Eder and D. Tambini (eds), *Citizenship, Markets and the State*, Oxford: Oxford University Press, 2001.

56 Department of Social Security, *A New Contract for Welfare*, Cm 3085, London: Stationery Office, 1998, p. 16.

57 Population Data Unit, *2001 UNHCR Population Statistics (Provisional)*, Geneva: UNHCR, 15 May 2002.

58 S. Lavenex, *The Europeanisation of Refugee Policies: Between Human Rights and Internal Security*, Aldershot: Ashgate, 2001.

59 P. 6, 'Tackling Social Exclusion and Unemployment: A Preliminary Assessment of New Labour's Approach in Britain', paper presented at Fondaçion Sistema Conference, Madrid, 3 December 1999.

60 Ibid.

61 B. Jordan, *The New Politics of Welfare: Social Justice in a Global Context*, London: Sage, 1998; R. Levitas, *The Inclusive Society? Social Exclusion and New Labour*, Basingstoke: Macmillan, 1998.

62 L.M. Mead, *Beyond Entitlement: The Social Obligations of Citizenship*, New York: Free Press, 1986; M.B. Katz, *The Undeserving Poor: From the War on Poverty to the War on Welfare*, New York: Pantheon, 1989.

63 See, for instance, A. Gutmann and D. Thompson, *Demo-*

cracy and Disagreement, Cambridge, MA: Harvard University Press, 1996; G. Standing, *Beyond the New Paternalism*, London: Verso, 2002.

64 For critiques of these regimes, see M. Dummett, *On Immigration and Refugees*, London: Routledge, 2001; T. Hayter, *Open Borders*, London: Pluto Press, 2000.

65 Department of Social Security, *A New Contract for Welfare*, p. 67.

66 Home Office, *Fairer, Faster and Firmer: A Modern Approach to Immigration and Asylum*, Cm 4018, London: Stationery Office, 1998.

67 Rawls, *A Theory of Justice*.

68 Sen, *Inequality Re-examined*.

69 Dworkin, 'What is Equality?'

70 G.A. Cohen, *Self-Ownership, Freedom and Equality*, Cambridge: Cambridge University Press, 1998.

71 B. Jordan with C. Jordan, *Social Work and the Third Way: Tough Love as Social Policy*, London: Sage, 2002.

Chapter 5 Global Equality and Justice

1 J. Rawls, *A Theory of Justice*, Oxford: Oxford University Press, 1971, p. 7.

2 Ibid., p. 9.

3 For instance, those of Owen, Godwin, Paine, Saint-Simon, Fourier, Proudhon and Weitling.

4 For instance, those of Bakunin, Kropotkin, Rocker, Nettlau and Serge.

5 M. Hollis, *The Philosophy of Social Science: An Introduction*, Cambridge: Cambridge University Press, 1994, p. 1.

6 For instance, Rawls, *A Theory of Justice*.

7 For instance, R. Dworkin, 'What is Equality? Part II: Equality of Resources', *Philosophy and Public Affairs*, 10, 1981, pp. 283–345; P. van Parijs, *Real Freedom for All: What (If Anything) Can Justify Capitalism?*, Oxford: Clarendon Press, 1995.

8 P. Cole, *Philosophies of Exclusion: Liberal Political Theory and*

Immigration, Edinburgh: Edinburgh University Press, 2000, pp. 193–5.

9 J. Rawls, *Political Liberalism*, New York: Columbia University Press, 1993, p. 277.

10 Ibid., p. 136.

11 J. Rawls, *The Law of Peoples*, Cambridge, MA: Harvard University Press, 1999, pp. 38–9.

12 Ibid., p. 39.

13 M. Walzer, *Spheres of Justice*, Oxford: Blackwell, 1983, pp. 39, 61–2.

14 J. Lewis, *The End of Marriage? Individualism and Intimate Relations*, Cheltenham: Edward Elgar, 2002.

15 G.K. Hadfield, 'Just Borders: Normative Economics and Immigration Law', in W.F. Schwartz (ed.), *Justice in Immigration*, Cambridge: Cambridge University Press, 1995, pp. 201–11, at p. 204.

16 N. Fraser, 'From Redistribution to Recognition? Dilemmas of Justice in a Post-Socialist Age', *New Left Review*, 212, 1995, pp. 68–93.

17 T. Hobbes, *Leviathan* (1651), ed. J. Plamenatz, London: Collins Fontana, 1962, p. 141.

18 Cole, *Philosophies of Exclusion*, chs 4 and 5.

19 Ibid., ch. 8.

20 R. Bauböck, *Transnational Citizenship: Membership and Rights in International Migration*, Aldershot: Edward Elgar, 1994, p. 171.

21 Ibid., pp. 14, 175.

22 H. Arendt, *Men in Dark Times*, San Diego: Harvest Books, 1970, pp. 81–2.

23 A.O. Sykes, 'The Welfare Economics of Immigration Law: A Theoretical Survey with Analysis of US Policy', in W.F. Schwartz (ed.), *Justice in Immigration*, Cambridge: Cambridge University Press, 1995, pp. 158–200, at pp. 160–1.

24 R. Boyer, 'The Political in an Era of Globalization and Finance: Focus on some *Régulation* School Research', *International Journal of Urban and Regional Research*, 24(2), 2000, pp. 275–322 at p. 311; E. Luttwak, *Turbo-capitalism:*

Winners and Losers in the Global Economy, New York: Weidenfeld and Nicolson, 1999, ch. 7.

25 B. Jordan, *A Theory of Poverty and Social Exclusion*, Cambridge: Polity, 1996, ch. 6.

26 Boyer, 'The Political in an Era of Globalization and Finance', p. 311.

27 Bauböck, *Transnational Citizenship*, p. 207.

28 Ibid., p. 210.

29 Ibid., p. 227.

30 Ibid.

31 Ibid.

32 T.H. Marshall, *Citizenship and Social Class*, Cambridge: Cambridge University Press, 1950; A. Sen, 'Capability and Wellbeing', in M. Nussbaum and A. Sen (eds), *The Quality of Life*, Oxford: Clarendon Press, 1993.

33 O. Blanchard, 'Labour Market Flexibility and Labour Market Institutions', paper presented at a conference, 'Beyond Transition', CASE Foundation, Warsaw, 12–13 April 2002.

34 A. Sen, 'Rights and Capabilities', in his *Resources, Values and Development*, Oxford: Blackwell, 1984, pp. 307–24.

35 See, for instance, T. Blair, Preface to Department of Social Security, *A New Contract for Welfare*, Cm 3805, London: Stationery Office, 1998, pp. i–iii.

36 P. 6, 'Welfare under Moral Scrutiny: Self-reliance, Paternalism, Preventing Intrusion and Moral Character', paper presented at a conference on 'The Morality of Welfare', St George's House, Windsor Castle, 27–29 June 1999.

37 R.H. Cox, 'From Safety Nets to Trampolines: Labour Market Activation in the Netherlands and Denmark', *Governance: An International Journal of Politics and Administration*, 11(4), 1998, pp. 397–414.

38 Department of Social Security, *A New Contract for Welfare*, p. 69.

39 Ibid.

40 Bauböck, *Transnational Citizenship*, p. 218.

41 Ibid., p. 290.

42 Ibid., p. 298.

43　A.B. Atkinson, *Public Economics in Action: The Basic Income/ Flat Tax Proposal*, Oxford: Oxford University Press, 1995.

44　B. Jordan, *The New Politics of Welfare: Social Justice in a Global Context*, London: Sage, 1998; van Parijs, *Real Freedom for All*; B. Barry, 'The Attractions of Basic Income', in J. Franklin (ed.), *Equality*, London: Institute for Public Policy Research, 1997, pp. 157–71; T. Fitzpatrick, *Freedom and Security: An Introduction to the Basic Income Debate*, London: Macmillan, 1999.

45　Jordan, *The New Politics of Welfare*; van Parijs, *Real Freedom for All*; Barry, 'The Attractions of Basic Income'; Fitzpatrick, *Freedom and Security*.

46　Bauböck, *Transnational Citizenship*; see also his 'The Crossing and Blurring of Boundaries in International Migration: Challenges for Social and Political Theory', in R. Bauböck and J. Rundell (eds), *Blurred Boundaries, Ethnicity, Citizenship*, Aldershot: Ashgate, 1998, pp. 17–52.

47　A. Casella and B. Frey, 'Federalism and Clubs: Towards an Economic Theory of Overlapping Political Jurisdictions', *European Economic Review*, 36(2/3), 1992, pp. 639–46, at p. 643.

48　T. Pogge, 'Interview: Globalising, with Justice', *Imprints: Journal of Analytical Socialism*, 5(3), 2001, pp. 199–220; T. Pogge, *World Poverty and Human Rights*, Cambridge: Polity, 2002.

49　Ibid.

50　C. McKinnon and I. Hampsher-Monk (eds), *The Demands of Citizenship*, London: Continuum, 2000.

51　Bauböck, *Transnational Citizenship*, p. 19.

52　Ibid., p. 219.

53　Ibid., ch. 4.

54　Ibid.

55　J. Locke, *Second Treatise of Government* (1698), ed. P. Laslett, Cambridge: Cambridge University Press, 1967, sec. 122.

56　Bauböck, *Transnational Citizenship*, pp. 86–92.

57　Ibid.

58　Ibid.

59 Ibid., pp. 167–8.
60 M. Joppke (ed.), *Challenge to the Nation State: Immigration in Western Europe and the United States*, Oxford: Oxford University Press, 1998.
61 B. Jordan and F. Düvell, *Irregular Migration: The Dilemmas of Transnational Mobility*, Cheltenham: Edward Elgar, 2002, ch. 2.
62 Bauböck, *Transnational Citizenship*, ch. 13.
63 Ibid., p. 19.
64 Ibid., p. 239.
65 Ibid., p. 230.
66 Ibid., p. 241.
67 Ibid.
68 Ibid., p. 245.
69 Rawls, *The Law of Peoples*, p. 26.
70 A. Revenko, 'Poor Strata of Population in Ukraine', paper presented at the Third International Conference on Social Problems, 'Social History of Poverty in Central Europe', Łodz: Poland, 3–6 December 1997.
71 B. Jordan with C. Jordan, *Social Work and the Third Way: Tough Love as Social Policy*, London: Sage, 2000, pp. 165–8.
72 World Bank, *World Development Report, 2000/2001: Attacking Poverty*, Washington, DC: World Bank/Oxford University Press, 2001.
73 Oxfam, 'Rigged Rules and Double Standards: Trade, Globalization and the Fight Against Poverty', press release, 24 April 2002; J.E. Stiglitz, *Globalization and Its Discontents*, London: Allen Lane, 2002, pp. 172–3, 176.
74 See Pogge, 'Interview: Globalising, with Justice'.

Index

activation   80–1, 98, 135
Afghanistan   66
Africa   42, 96
  Horn of   66
  North   76, 111
  sub-Saharan   64
agriculture   41–2, 66, 82,
    150, 153
Algeria   65
America
  Central   74
  Latin   39–40, 96
  North   60, 72–3
amnesties   67, 77, 79, 88
Amsterdam   74, 84
anti-globalization movement
    33, 59–60
Argentina   39–40
Aristotle   50
Arrow, Kenneth   38
Asia   42, 96
  Central   65
  East   39, 69–74, 84
  migration system in
    69–72

refugees in   64
South-East   7, 37, 71
associations   17, 77, 85–6,
    94–5, 97, 102, 105–8,
    110–11, 130–4, 136,
    153
  voluntary   12, 130–1
asylum   17–19, 23–6,
    59–61, 63–4, 66, 68–9,
    76, 83, 85–6, 90, 98,
    114–19, 120, 133,
    145–6, 150
Australia   3, 6, 24, 60, 67,
    71, 73–4

Baltic States   65
Bangladesh   57
banks   33, 40–1, 113
basic income   26, 129,
    137–43, 147–9, 152,
    155
Bauböck, Rainer   138,
    143–8
begging   98
Belgium   84

Berlin 79–80
Blair, Tony 16
boundaries 3, 9–14, 17, 24,
    26–32, 40–1, 54–5,
    57–8, 90–5, 111–13,
    119, 121, 125–6,
    128–32
Bradford 111
'brain drain' 2, 81
Brazil 39, 57
bureaucrats 34
Burma 67
Burnley 111
business visas 88–9

Canada 6, 71
capabilities 21, 45, 107–11,
    116, 121, 134–5
  defined 107
Cape Town 25
carers 71, 80, 102, 104,
    126, 130, 136
Caribbean countries 65, 72,
    74
Chile 38
China 36–8, 57, 100
  migration from 60, 70
cities 46, 86, 102–5, 111
  in federalism 50–1
  free 48
  global 63, 70–1, 103–4,
    131
citizenship 19–25, 50, 53,
    62, 64, 66, 90–123, 132,
    134, 136, 138–43
  access to 120, 142–9
  active 131

dual 75–7, 145–6
  obligations of 99, 133
  renunciation of 143–9
civic republicanism 50,
    107–8, 131
clubs 13–14, 29, 31, 54–5,
    57–8, 61, 93, 102, 109,
    139–40, 142, 149
  theory of 3, 12
Cohen, G.A. 119
Cold War 124
collective goods 11–14,
    19–20, 22, 28–32,
    44–58, 99, 109–21, 139
colonialism 48, 62, 104,
    120
Common Agricultural Policy
    145
communal systems 9, 43–4,
    56–7, 61, 63, 74, 99,
    149–50, 154
communitarianism 92, 130,
    146
communities 45–6, 56, 62,
    85, 130
  of choice 31, 93–5, 104,
    109–13, 117, 122
  ethical 92
  of fate 31, 103, 122–3,
    146, 149–54
  transnational 75–8
Cooper, Robert 16
co-operation 4
Copenhagen 85
corporations, *see* firms
credit
  international 23

crime   2, 12, 18, 24, 36, 75,
    97–8, 122, 150–1
  international   18, 101,
    150–1
Cuba   101

debt   33, 42, 154
defence   11, 25
democratic principles   17,
    19–20, 23, 30, 35, 38,
    43, 50, 53–5, 68–9,
    90–9, 105, 130–1, 134,
    141–2, 145, 155
Denmark   3
dependence   23, 40, 78,
    116–17, 123, 132, 135
detention centres   114, 118,
    127
developing countries   3,
    5–6, 8–9, 14, 28, 30–1,
    33, 37–8, 41–7, 53–8,
    60, 62, 67, 70–3, 78, 81,
    99, 137, 149–54
diasporas   76
dictatorship   38
disabilities   23
domestic service workers
    71, 79
'dragon economies'   71–2
drug abuse   122, 151
drug trafficking   16, 19, 101,
    150–1
Dworkin, Ronald   119

education   12–14, 21, 54,
    61, 80, 84, 86, 88, 98,
    108, 111–13, 116, 130,
    134, 136, 152–3
  for asylum seekers   114
  for citizenship   144
  qualifications of migrants
    25, 72, 81
elderly people   102, 126–7,
    132
emancipation   3–4
empowerment   44–6, 51,
    55, 112
environment   1, 32, 41–3,
    149
  protection of   11, 50,
    53–4, 124, 139, 149
'ethical perspective'   14–15,
    17, 19–20, 33, 59–60,
    91–9, 124, 137, 148
  defined   3
Europe   7, 15, 73–4, 84, 87,
    97, 114, 118
  Central and Eastern   18,
    36–7, 57, 60, 72
  emigration from   65
  'Fortress'   18
  medieval   48
  in migration systems   60,
    74
  northern   65, 79
  southern   67, 79
  subsidiarity in   49
European Commission   18,
    68
European Monetary Union
    39
European Union (EU)   18,
    29, 36, 141

enlargement of   39
free movement in
     114–15, 145
immigration policies in
     68, 114–15
irregular migrants in   67
exchange rates   39
exclusion   11–13, 51, 55,
     93–5, 99–100, 105,
     109–11, 119, 121, 126,
     129–32, 153–4
exit   4, 23, 31
  rights of   6, 109–13,
     126–7, 142–3
  rules for   4
externalities   2, 51, 94–5, 98
  defined   2

failure
  government   30, 32–6, 41,
     150
  market   30, 32–6, 150
  moral   98
families   9, 18, 61, 63, 74,
     76, 81, 85–6, 102,
     111–12, 122, 126, 130,
     132, 136
  reunification of   115
famine   63, 150
'federalist perspective'
     10–14, 17–21, 27–9,
     47–55, 57–9, 91, 128–9,
     137–8, 140
  defined   3
firms   6–8, 10–14, 23,
     29–30, 33–6, 61, 73, 78,

     80, 82, 102, 110, 112,
     117, 119, 127, 132
  foreign recruitment by   8,
     70–1, 80–1, 84–90
  small   39–40, 70, 74–5,
     77–8, 154
fiscal federalism   3, 12–14,
     28–9, 46–55, 139
Fortuyn, Pim   115–16
France   66, 76, 101, 111,
     115–16

Gdansk   85
gender   6, 94, 97–8, 114,
     122
General Agreement on Trade
     in Services (GATS)   3,
     13–14, 25, 58, 154
'globalist perspective'
     13–15, 17–19, 21, 27–8,
     33–47, 55–9, 78, 91,
     128–9, 137–9, 147
  defined   3
governance
  corporate   39–40
  global   27–32, 76, 80–1,
     83, 89, 91, 99–100, 109,
     116–17, 121, 135,
     139–40, 149, 151–4
  of poverty   41–7
Greece   65, 80

Haass, Richard   15
health care   12–14, 21, 25,
     54, 84, 88, 93, 98,
     108–9, 111–13, 116,
     129, 134, 136, 152

health care (*cont.*)
  for asylum seekers   114
Hirschman, A.O.   23
Hobbes, Thomas   3, 22,
  125–6
Hong Kong   37, 70
  migration to   71, 74
human rights   50, 72, 128,
  138–43, 156
  UN Declaration of   41
Hungary   153
Hussein, Saddam   42

imperialism   16, 104
  economic   40
income distribution   3, 6,
  21, 44, 49, 53–4, 69, 96,
  98, 104–5, 107–8, 116,
  118, 128–9, 137, 139,
  145
income security   134–6, 155
India   24, 60, 71
  migrants from   84–90
Indonesia   70–1
informal economic activity
  9, 43, 61–2, 73–8, 111,
  149–54
infrastructure   8, 12–14, 25,
  28–9, 47–55, 59, 78, 83,
  93, 103–4, 110, 112–13,
  121, 133, 139–40,
  152–3, 155
International Development
  Association (IDA)
  56–8, 100–1
International Labour Office
  18

International Monetary Fund
  (IMF)   2, 7, 9, 15, 27,
  30, 32–47, 56–8, 94,
  99–100
International Organization for
  Migration (IOM)   2, 18
Iraq   24, 42
irregular migration   25–6,
  67–8, 74–5, 77–83, 86,
  88, 103–4, 115–16, 120
Israel   66
Istanbul   84
Italy   66, 80, 101

Japan   7, 70–1

Keynesianism   44
Kurds   24, 76, 85–6
Kuwait   65

labour markets   27–8, 32,
  40, 81–2, 87–90, 105,
  117, 133, 135–6, 154
  flexibility in   37, 42, 68,
    70, 80–1, 89
  in migration systems
    70–1
  recruitment of skilled
    workers   68, 154
  regulation of   68, 75, 78–9
  transnational   74–6, 87–8
land   30–1, 37, 43, 102,
  104–5, 125
  development of   47–8,
    57–9
  redistribution of   46
  as social dividend   137

law 91, 125
  and order 11
Le Pen, Jean-Marie 115–16
Leviathan 49
liberal democracy 6, 17, 62,
    68, 72, 90–9, 105–6,
    109–11, 114–23, 128,
    131, 134, 144
liberalism 20, 22, 91–8,
    106–13, 125, 134, 145,
    148
  historical 97
  neo- 20
local authorities 49–55,
    57–8
location-specific advantages
    62, 77
  defined 77
Locke, John 125, 144
London 24, 74–5, 79–80,
    84–5
loyalty 23, 31
Luxembourg 66

Maastricht Treaty 18
Machiavelli, Nicolò 22
Malaysia 70–1
marriage 79, 98
Mediterranean region 60
  migration from 65
membership systems 2–5,
    9–14, 17, 21–4, 27–32,
    44–55, 61–2, 75–8, 128,
    149–54
  economic 26, 29, 51–5,
    61, 83–7, 93–121
  transnational 76–8

welfare states as 6, 21, 96
Mexico 57
Middle East 72
'migration crisis' 64–9
minorities 2
  ethnic 4, 25, 62, 72–8,
    80, 111, 121–2, 132
Montenegro 39
Montesquieu, Charles 50
Morocco 65
Mozambique 66–7
Mugabe, Robert 42

'nationalist perspective' 13,
    15–17, 19, 35, 59–62,
    125, 128–9, 132–3,
    137–8, 141–2, 148
  defined 3
needs 94–6, 98, 109, 127,
    130, 134–5
Neighbourhood Watch 111
Netherlands 3, 115–16
New Labour 49
New Zealand 6, 57
nomadism 22, 26, 60–1,
    83–7, 127, 138, 141–2,
    144, 154
  defined 61
  elite 71–2
non-government
  organizations (NGOs)
    3, 14–15, 23, 33, 44–6,
    99, 153
North Korea 101
Northern Ireland 111
Nozick, Robert 20
nursing 86

Oldham 111
oligarchs 40–1
oligopoly 6–7, 12, 127
Oman 65
organizations 3, 6, 10–14,
    26, 28–32, 42, 45–55,
    75, 91–9, 125, 128, 131
  defined 4
  economic 5, 10–15,
    29–31

Pakistan 25, 60
Palestinians 64, 66
pauperism 97
pensions 8
  funds 23, 25, 56, 93,
    109
people smuggling 101, 151
persecution 22
Philippines 67, 70–1
Pinochet, Augusto 38
Plato 50
Poland 24, 36
  migrants from 74–5, 80,
    84–90
police 18, 151
poor people 2, 19, 23, 33,
    41–7, 52, 55, 104, 111,
    121–3, 149–54
  exclusion of 55, 105,
    109–10
  migration by 60
  networks of 46
Portugal 66
post-communist countries
    9, 14, 39–40, 53, 57, 78,
    81, 99, 151–2

poverty 28, 30, 36, 41–55,
    97, 123
  reduction 33, 100
Poverty Reduction Strategy
    Papers 57, 100
Powell, Colin 15
power 15–19, 23, 30, 38,
    44–7, 94, 130, 134–5,
    140, 146
  financial 40
  of international
    organizations 33
  monopoly 34
  patriarchal 97, 132
prison 123, 133, 151
property rights 93–4, 97,
    123, 133, 147
  shareholders' 39–40
public choice 10–14,
    47–55, 109
public goods 11, 32, 50–1
public services 3, 6, 10–14,
    25, 34, 49–55, 58, 78,
    83, 104–21, 133, 152–5
  professionals in 25, 86
  public–private partnerships
    14, 29, 44
  recruitment abroad for
    86–7
public sphere 105–9, 121,
    134
punishment 97–8, 123

Qatar 65

'race' 6, 17, 62, 94, 97,
    111, 114–16, 122, 156

rationality 96–9
Rawls, John 20, 91, 96, 119, 125, 148
regularization, *see* amnesties
religious groups 76–7, 138
remittances 74, 76–7
'rent seeking' 34–5, 38
  defined 34
Roma 153
Rousseau, Jean-Jacques 50, 125
Russia 25, 36–40, 101

Saudi Arabia 65
Scandinavia 7
sedentary lifestyles 62, 76–8, 94, 104–5, 126–7, 135, 141–3, 154, 156
Sen, Amartya 107, 119
Seoul 71
settlement 62, 64, 66, 76, 78–9, 104, 144–9
sex workers 71, 79
shareholders 30, 39–40
Singapore 70, 101
slavery 97
Slovakia 37
Smith, Adam 11
social assistance 74, 98, 117–18, 125
social capital 45–6, 50, 63, 74, 77, 85, 132, 147
social citizenship 6, 10, 72, 116, 127
social contract 44, 118, 125, 148
social goods 26, 128

social insurance 7, 79, 82
social justice 3, 13, 19–24, 124, 138, 140, 142, 155
'social partners' 7
social protection 2, 6, 8, 34, 36, 44, 53–5, 127, 133
social reproduction 31, 102, 130
socialism 152–4
  state 5, 9, 37, 65–6, 153
Somalia 67
South Africa 67
South Korea 70
sovereignty 1, 15–19, 50–1, 91, 97, 106, 120
Soviet Bloc 35
Soviet Union 36, 57, 64–6
sports clubs 28, 85, 88
Stalinism 66
Stiglitz, Joseph 15, 33–6, 38
Structural and Cohesion Funds 145
students 16, 63, 79–80, 103, 120
Sudan 67
Sussex 24
Switzerland 51, 66

Taipei 70
Taiwan 70, 74
tariffs 35
tax credits 135–7
taxation 8, 22, 24, 37, 49, 53–4, 68, 74–5, 88, 106, 108–10, 112–13, 117, 123, 137–8

telecommunications 11–12, 40

territory 5, 17, 43, 47–55, 59, 105, 121, 125, 130

terrorism 15–16, 19, 41, 103

Thailand 70–1

Third Way 133

Tiebout, Charles 51–2

Tobin tax 22, 140, 155

Tokyo 70–1

tourism 63–4, 79, 103, 120, 144

trade 27–8, 32, 48, 51, 71, 74, 76–7, 83, 96, 120, 154–5

trade unions 6–7, 14, 34–5, 73–4, 127

trafficking
of drugs, *see* drug trafficking
of people 18, 101

transnationalism 73–8

transport 13, 48, 62, 75, 98
public 108, 143

Treasury (US) 10, 15, 33, 38

'tropical capitalism' 74

Tunisia 65

Turkey 65
migrants from 74–6, 85–6

Ukraine 36

unemployment 36–7, 61, 81, 116–17

insurance 81–2

United Kingdom (UK) 6–7, 14, 24–5, 57, 101–2, 111, 115, 118–19, 123, 135–7
emigration from 65, 71
migration to 60, 66, 79, 84
public sector reforms in 29, 49, 54, 113

United Nations (UN) 128, 141

United States of America (USA) 7, 14–19, 28, 35, 49, 57, 101–2, 111, 117, 123, 128
investment from 70
irregular migrants in 67, 79
migration to 65, 67, 74, 84, 86–7
Treasury 10, 15, 33, 38
workfare in 117–18, 135, 137

Uruguay 39

Vienna 84

Vietnam 101

voice 23, 31, 94, 110, 142

voting 108, 139, 142, 145
with the feet 52, 58, 109

wages 8, 56, 69, 86–7, 132
inequality of 70, 77
minimum 25, 82, 135–7
supplementation of 135–7

Walzer, Michael   125
war   2, 9, 24, 32, 59, 63,
   125
   civil   42, 66–7, 101, 150
warlords   101, 150
Washington Consensus   3,
   15, 20, 28, 32
welfare states   6–9, 10–14,
   32, 80–2, 96, 106,
   127–8, 132–4, 138, 140,
   146, 156
women   3, 71, 79–80, 94,
   97–8, 126–7, 132
   subordination of   97
work enforcement   23, 37,
   80, 98, 117, 123, 127,
   131, 135–7
   in workhouses   97

work permits   24, 86, 88,
   118–19
World Bank   2, 7, 9, 21, 23,
   27–8, 30, 32–47, 56–8,
   94, 99–100, 153
World Trade Center   103
World Trade Organization
   (WTO)   2, 13–14,
   27–8, 32–47, 57, 94

xenophobia   115

Yugoslavia
   Federal Republic of   39
   former   64–6

Zimbabwe   42